Copyright © 2020 Dick Bell, Seaton, Devon.

Written by Dick Bell MBE
Designed and edited by P. F. Adams

Scripture quotations [marked NIV] taken from the Holy Bible,
New International Version Anglicised Copyright © 1979, 1984, 2011 Biblica

Used by permission of Hodder & Stoughton Ltd, an Hachette UK Company

All rights Reserved

'NIV' is a registered trademark of Biblica UK trademark number 1448790.

Two Trees Series

First published in 2020 by Dick Bell MBE

Walking by the Holy Spirit

by Dick Bell MBE

Contents

Prologue:

Walking by the Holy Spirit.

There is a chapter in my first book about the Bible. But not in these consequent books. Therefore, please hear something about the Bible, because this little book is all about what the Bible tells us.

The Bible is Absolute Truth. Jesus (God) is different – He is Complete Truth. So, for example, the Bible will not be able to tell you whether to have cereal or bacon and egg for breakfast this morning. But Jesus can and will. The Bible is absolutely true, but not the whole truth.

What God has done is to take selected portions of truth from earth's ages and written them down for us all. Each portion, God thinks, is useful for all mankind as a means of getting in touch with Jesus, who is the whole truth. So, the Bible is absolutely true in every part. It says of itself *"All Scripture is God-breathed and is useful for teaching, rebuking, correcting and training in righteousness,"* (2 Tim 3:16). So, please do not despise or reject any of it.

It is the very best means whereby you can find the whole truth – Jesus. The Bible tells us how to find Him: Jesus alone can set us free.

There are those Christians who get stuck in their Bibles. They are faithful, loyal and reliable. But they have not yet branched out from their Bibles into the glorious freedom and liberty that is the hallmark of Walking in the Spirit – as their Bibles tell them to do. They are, in fact, under law – the law of the Bible. Our Bibles are wonderful guides to heaven, but are not heaven itself.

Most Bible teachers recommend that we read our Bibles daily. I agree – that is a good strategy. But do not learn what it says – listen to the Holy Spirit as you read it. Jesus said that the Holy Spirit would be our teacher (John 14:26): the Bible is not our teacher. The Bible is a channel, a means through which God can communicate personally with us. God in Jesus is the most important Man in the universe; He is omnipresent to all of us; He is the great lover who is wooing us to live with Him in heaven. Jesus is the purpose, the means, the method and the end of the universe. All things were made by Him and for Him (Col 1). The Spirit alone brings Life. The Bible is dead without Him. If you have been spoken to through the Bible, you have been spoken to by the Holy Spirit. Believe, receive, analyse how He did it, and then multiply that method.

Now I pray that my revelations on aspects of the Bible in this little book will teach you more about Jesus, fill you with more joy than so far you have ever experienced, and bring you into great reconciliation with yourself, God's world, other people and with God Himself.

Rescue.

God's Rescue is generally called Salvation. I use the word Rescue because it is less Christian jargon. So why does the Bible use it so much?

It describes the most beautiful thing that God has done for mankind. He has offered to every human being on earth the opportunity to fulfil the destiny God planned for each of us when He made us. There really is a Divine purpose in being alive, and in being who we are.

None of us knows that we even need rescuing. "I'm OK; why should I need rescuing?" we think. Most people struggle through life, but generally we are content with what we have and who we are. We just do not realise that living an ordinary human life until we die is a disaster of immeasurable proportions.

Few of us realises that we have been taken over by God's vicious and ruthless enemy – but we all have been. None of us are what we should be. Satan, God's undying enemy, makes sure that we are anaesthetised by tranquillity and blinded concerning our eternal destiny.

So what is the problem?

Sin; which matters supremely to God. The Trinity is perfect in all they think and do, totally dependent on each other in love for ever. Sin is diametrically opposite to that – independent, self-centred, self-indulgent and proud. No big ME can fit into God's Kingdom, God's heaven or God's company. *Every* little wickedness matters. *Every* decision made without God is sin. That makes every human being black from God's perspective: none can enter His heaven. Not one qualifies.

That is a huge problem to us all (and we need to be aware of it). But it also a huge problem to God Himself. He made us in love to live with Him eternally, and none qualify. We all live in satan's kingdom, qualifying for eternal hell – designed for satan and his demons. We are born bent, and from our earliest days we confirm that bentness by doing stupid, selfish things. Straight away we destine ourselves for eternal fire and punishment. Even parents know that stupidity and disobedience in their children must be punished. In the same way, God punishes disobedience. Going to hell when we die is *Just* in God's sight. It is inevitable and unavoidable for us all. We are, after all, privileged creatures – the greatest that God has so far made and Lords of earth.

God's rescue package for mankind was exceedingly complicated. It had to satisfy God's Righteousness and Justice as well as His Love. His love insisted on devising a rescue. His Justice could only be solved righteously by Him, the Judge of all, taking on the consequent punishment Himself. But it had to be righteous, indeed perfect. How? God Himself had to become a human being and pay the price of disobedience on your behalf. Yours.

It is individual. He died for *you*. God does not want *you* to go to hell and to spend the rest of eternity carrying the consequences of your own foolishnesses. God has got a marvellous heaven prepared for all mankind, and, without His rescue package in Jesus, it will be empty for ever. God wants you to enjoy His eternal beauty, bliss and paradise and become Royalty with Him over the whole of the rest of creation. That is mankind's destiny. That is why Jesus came to rescue you from the devastating consequences of your blind, selfish life on earth.

Not even God is sovereign over Himself. That is why there is a Trinity; they are so submitted to each other in love that only together can They rule over the universe. Accessing God's salvation starts, therefore, with you surrendering your own sovereignty to the Three of them. This life and body you have was given to you as a gift in the first place. Now, stop clinging to it as if you own it, and hand it over to the beautiful God who blessed you with it. Do not be afraid: He is quite safe. But you cannot join the Trinity until you are like them – utterly dependent on Them.

The rescue package contains not only a "from" but also a "to". I am being rescued *from* a dead life of nothingness and rescued *to* a real life of everythingness. If you like, it is a detailed and very careful rearrangement of the gungy mess inside the chrysalis that is your life to a life of order, beauty, and butterfly. Paul caught God's heart precisely; *"He has delivered us out of the power of darkness, and translated us into the Kingdom of the Son of his love."* (Col 1:13 ASV).

Rescue emphasises the "from" more than the "to". Salvation is both. And brilliant.

So how do we access Jesus' Rescue Package in the Now?

> "Riches I heed not, nor man's empty praise.
>
> Thou my inheritance now and always.
>
> Christ of my own heart, whatever befall
>
> Be thou my vision, thou Ruler of all."

Is Jesus not called Saviour? That means He does it all. He is the personal surgeon that slices off every ugly cancer from our souls, picked up in our past from bad people, bad habits and bad decisions. He is also the personal Provider through His Holy Spirit who rebuilds us and re-forms us into good, honest, honourable, reliable citizens, Sons of the Most High God, Princes and Princesses in the Kingdom of heaven. It cannot even begin without your surrender to His love. Let go and let God.

The rescue of Jesus Christ is fully, continually, thoroughly, perfectly and extravagantly effective to bring each of us out of the messy chrysalis we were born into and be remade into a beautiful butterfly that can fly for ever in God's good heaven. *That's* salvation.

God's Strategic Plan.

God has a plan for the universe. Here it is.

What is God's aim – His ultimate goal? To have an enormous physical creation that works perfectly. This present one will not do – man has ruined it. So He is going to create a New Heaven and a New Earth, replacing this present one. What He is going to do with the new one and in it I have little idea. But it will be bigger and better than the one you and I are living in at present. It *has to be* perfect. So all the workers would be perfect and uniquely fulfilling their designed roles in whatever form and God Himself (the Trinity being the only perfect and complete Beings in existence) can direct and control the whole. It will be easy for Him (Them) to do that; They are, after all, quietly and covertly doing that in this creation.

This is how it all panned out from the beginning.

Firstly, God had to build His universe. Secondly, He had to plan workers. To set it up, He introduced angelic beings (spirit beings) to oversee every heavenly body (stars, planets, galaxies etc) on His behalf. Because He had planned that the earth should be the central focus of this present creation, He put His most important Being in charge to supervise this earth. His name was (is) Lucifer, the Morning Star. We learn from the Bible that Lucifer was the most important of all heavenly beings – the Guardian Cherub. So Lucifer would be the perfect communicator between God and earth, to bring all the creatures of earth in line with God's perfect and delightful character and will.

So this earth and this cosmos are the field-test, the fore-runner, the trial scenario for His strategic plan. Being God, He made this one perfect. He also constructed mankind perfectly. (Perhaps (only perhaps), He had in mind this cosmos to be the only one, depending on whether mankind preferred His way to satan's).

Then God made man. Man was (and is) God's most magnificent creation. They had to be physical as well as spiritual, otherwise they could not control a physical universe. So He had to make them magnificent, fit to rule over the animals and environment of earth. There is an old Pharisaic tradition that says that Lucifer objected to God's plan to make mankind the highest creatures in the cosmos, even greater than all the angels. Mankind was to be both physical and spiritual. Lucifer's rebellious thoughts were discovered, and he became instantly and totally dark, and was renamed satan or the devil (the accuser). He was thrown out of heaven. One third of all the other angels decided to follow him, and were themselves cast down to earth.

God still had a purpose for them all, and did not change their basic remit, which was to be carriers of salvation to those humans who were to be God's heirs (Heb 1:14).

Lucifer remained the angelic being in charge of earth. But now he was not able to pass on God's instructions to man, so he only passed on his own. He recognised that God had given mankind all authority over the earth. So if he was going to change the earth to line up with his will rather than God's, he was going to have to get mankind on his side. Fortunately, God had given mankind the same will as Lucifer and all the other angels had – to make their own decisions and choose their own destinies. So, very carefully, Lucifer made a move to persuade mankind to be on his side rather than God's. He cleverly chose the weaker of the only two then existing – the lady Eve (she had probably not been with Adam when God gave him the prohibition not to eat the fruit of the tree of the Knowledge of Good and Evil). She did not get it fully right anyway. She succumbed to Lucifer's selfish temptation and ate the forbidden fruit. Adam then had a terrible choice – to follow God or to follow his wife. Since she was the only creature on earth to whom he could relate perfectly, Adam chose Eve's way, and ate the forbidden fruit, the consequence of which was death. At that moment Adam introduced death to himself and to the whole of God's good creation.

So God's original plan failed: mankind from then on would follow his own and satan's way, and not God's. They and the whole earth would from then on be a failure. But God is never defeated; He is never lost for solutions. He loved His creation, so, in order to retain it, He had to redeem it – or at least redeem mankind, God's best creation. There was no creature in the cosmos who could redeem that for Him; both the angels and mankind had proven to be failures. So He had to do it Himself. Hence Jesus, the God-Man. Hence also the cross.

Like a little boy pulling the wings and legs off a fly while it is still alive just for his personal pleasure, so mankind has poisoned and polluted God's good earth and fouled it for ever, just for our personal pleasure – just for fun. Earth is no longer fit for God's original purpose, so He now uses it to bring wicked mankind to Himself. Because man had fouled up God's good earth, God uses its mess to bring people to Himself. Those self-centred humans who desired to know Him, God redeems from their sins and brings them into a personal relationship with Him. But He leaves them on earth to cement their choice of relationship to Him by giving them hassle every day. What God was looking for was a bunch of physical/spiritual creatures who would be prepared to go through any kind of trouble to qualify to help Him run His New Heavens and New Earth for Him. So today's earth is God's "School of Hard Knocks" for heaven.

God's plan will be completed when He has enough friends to fulfil every function in His New Creation. He will then bring this creation to an end. He will burn up earth with fire and wrap up the heavens like a scroll. He will create new "resurrection" bodies for His followers, so that they can be fully equipped to live in a physical/spiritual environment with perfect, flawless and blameless bodies, and not just be spirits.

What He has in mind for the New Creation to do after that, He has not revealed to anyone yet. What we do know is that *"God's dwelling-place is (will be) now among the people, and he will dwell with them. They will be his people, and God himself will be with them and be their God. He will wipe every tear from their eyes. There will be no more death or mourning or crying or pain, for the old order of things has passed away. He who was seated on the throne said, 'I am making everything new!'"* (Rev 21:3-5).

That is His Strategic Plan. Fitting in with it seems to me to be the most important thing a human being can ever consider doing. What is your strategic plan for your life after you die?

The Gospel.

Most people will know that the word Gospel means Good News. And mostly it applies to the Good News that Jesus Christ came to bring.

So what is this Good News?

Let me summarise it first, and then develop it so that you can see just how it works out.

Jesus Christ, by His death on the cross 2000 years ago, has set mankind free from:

1. A lifestyle governed by self-determination. That is – from sin and all its guilt.

2. The authority of Law with all its rules and regulations. And all its bondage.

3. Death, and all its terrors.

Jesus has replaced those three with the one Holy Spirit. And then added righteousness.

In a nutshell, that is the Gospel. So let me unravel each of those separately.

A Lifestyle Governed by Self-determination.

Let me begin at the beginning, and here I have to refer to the Bible as the source of my understanding.

The first man Adam and his wife Eve were perfect in every respect. So exceptional were they that they were told to go and subdue the earth (Gen 1:28). We have no reason to believe that that meant anything less than the whole earth. So they must have been amazing in their ability, their intelligence, their skills and their ability to do all the replenishing that was necessary. They did this without difficulty. We know that because, after they had sinned, Adam was punished by having to work by sweating (Gen 3:19). So, clearly, he worked before without sweat. That is, without effort.

Adam and Eve were told not to eat of the fruit of the tree of the Knowledge of Good and Evil. But they were tempted by satan and did. God had warned them that the consequence of eating that fruit was death. It is doubtful if they understood the extent of what death meant, but they found out soon enough after they had disobeyed and eaten. To summarise those consequences, it meant doing everything from then on in their own strength. They had chosen to leave God out of their lives, so they were forced into a lifestyle of self-determination.

So man and mankind (Adam and Eve and all of their descendants) now had to live on the earth with every kind of restraint and limitation. Everything became an effort. And everything man does is dead.

Why is that latter statement true?

From the day Adam disobeyed God until today mankind has created his own lifestyle. Because he needed to eat and because he needed shelter, he had to do something. So, from his own initiative, little by little he constructed the world systems that we now live in. We too have to eat, and the only way we have of getting food is to belong inside mankind's culture and lifestyle of death.

This lifestyle of self-determination God calls Sin. Self-determination is an endemic sickness throughout mankind (indeed, born into every human being), and is destroying the world on which man depends for his survival. He is fouling his own nest. All his efforts are death and dead.

Even his righteousness is wicked. Even though good deeds look good to us and to those who do them, they don't look good to God, who knows that they are motivated from a self-centred root. If the root is not dealt with by Jesus, then nothing, absolutely nothing that anyone does can possibly please God. Therefore it is still sin. The Bible says that even our righteousness is like a used sanitary towel (translators are kind – they translate it "filthy rags" in Isaiah 64:6).

Now let me briefly follow the consequences of this self-determination.

Adam's children had nothing to stop them sinning. So everybody did what was right in their own eyes, and the consequent wickedness over c.1800 years was so awful that God was sorry that He had made man and destroyed them all through a global Flood (Gen 6:5-8). Only eight were rescued, along with pairs of animals and birds. Then God started again.

So what, for Noah's children and grandchildren, restrained them from doing the evil that their predecessors had done?

Law.

The first thing that God did for Noah and his three sons was to give them rules by which they might live (Gen 9:1-6). Along with those rules God gave them a conscience so that it hurt inside when they broke the rules.

So let me summarise what Jesus did on the cross in relation to man's self-determined sin.

Jesus lived the whole of His life in total obedience to God. That is, without making any selfish personal decisions – without sin or sins. He was born with the same restricted body that we have (that is, not like Adam's original super body), and went to the cross still in obedience to His Father. On that cross, *"God made him who had no sin, to be sin for us, that we might be made the righteousness of God in him."* (2 Cor 5:21). Jesus then selected the death of His body; He deliberately gave up His spirit (John 10:17-18. John 19:30), and incorporated the removal of both sin and death in that action. God took that death of His Son as punishment for the whole of mankind. The first Adam bequeathed sin to all mankind: the second Adam (Jesus) neutralised it all, and bequeathed eternal Life to all who would surrender to Him. Thus, in principle, the whole of mankind has been set free from both their self-determining lifestyle and the consequences of it. But it only becomes effective as individuals surrender to Jesus. 1 Cor 15:45 *"So it is written: "The first man Adam became a living being"; the last Adam, a life-giving spirit."*

The Authority of Law with all its Rules and Regulations.

As I have said, God gave Noah and his sons law after they had vacated the Ark. So why law? What does law do? The New Testament gives us three very clear reasons why law was imposed on mankind:

1. The foremost purpose of law is to highlight man's wickednesses. Through the law comes knowledge of sin. (Rom 3:20)

2. To restrain evil (Gal 3:23). Through conscience and punishment, law stops man getting as bad as our antediluvian (pre-flood) ancestors were.

3. To bring people to Christ (Gal 3:24). *"So the law was our guardian until Christ came that we might be justified by faith."* The law is perfect in its demands. No human is perfect or anywhere near. Therefore man gets frustrated with his

inadequacies and turns to Jesus in his desperation to ask for forgiveness and rescue.

Summarising that: Law tells us we are bad, stops us getting worse and leads us to Christ. Self-determining man cannot avoid law. God placed law inseparably inside man's psyche and society. Rebellion of any kind is called anarchy (and is what the antediluvians were perfect at).

All these things were in God's hands. It was the only thing (and the very best thing) that God could do to stop the anarchy that occurred before the Flood. It established a system that sinful man could live under, but it never dealt with the root of his wickedness – the self-determination and independence of his nature.

Man has taken the gift of Law from God, misunderstood it completely, and twisted it to his advantage. The authorities inundate societies with more and more laws, hoping that they will bring those societies into greater and greater righteousness. Instead, it brings them into greater and greater despair. Or rebellion.

So now let me tackle what Jesus has done about the law. I need to rely on the Bible to show you, because most people have trouble believing what the Bible says.

It says that Jesus has abolished the law with its rules and regulations. (Eph 2:14-15).

So those who access the salvation (rescue) that Jesus offers have been set free from the supervision of the law (Gal 3:25). Law no longer controls them (Rom 7:5). They are not "under" the law for their lifestyle or behaviour (Rom 6:14). Law must no longer set a pattern for their lives (Rom 7:1-4). By observing the law no one will be made good (Rom 3:20). If righteousness could be gained through the law, then Christ died for nothing (Gal 2:21). All who rely on observing the law are under a curse (Gal 3:10). *"You who are trying to be justified by law have been alienated from Christ; you have fallen away from grace."* (Gal 5:4).

Instead, God has replaced law by the Holy Spirit, who controls, guides and directs Christians' lives for them. In that way every Christian who obeys the Holy Spirit pleases God in every way and obeys all of God's laws, which are far higher than man's laws and incorporate many of man's laws. Indeed, Jesus told His followers that unless their righteousness exceeded that of the scribes and Pharisees, they would never enter heaven (Matt 5:20).

Jesus Himself disobeyed some of the laws of the land when He lived on earth, particularly the Sabbath laws that the rulers had conjured up. He said they were made by man and not by God. And at one point he confronted His accusers and asked, *"Can any of you prove me guilty of sin?"* (John 8:46). No one could answer.

The Apostle Paul wrote his letter to the Galatians for this one express purpose – to tell them to stop living by the law, and to put their faith in Jesus instead, and live by the Holy Spirit. Living by human law was sin. Indeed, *"Everything that does not come from faith is sin."* (Rom 14:23b).

So how does this work out in practice? How can a Christian live in this man-determined world which is governed by laws, rules and regulations, and yet not be "under" law?

The Bible answer is very simple: God is writing *His laws in their hearts*, (Jer 31:33) so that, obeying the Holy Spirit means that we will never be led wrong. The Spirit's promptings lead us into deeds and actions that no law on earth can touch. Indeed, the fruit of the Spirit in Galatians 5:22-23 says "against such there is no law."

God is creating a brand-new kind of human being inside the old body that Christians were born with. He starts with establishing our relationship with Jesus, who becomes a personal friend. He then goes on to remove all the vestiges of our old selfish, independent lifestyle one by one, and replaces them in us with a new creation that is a copy of Jesus' lifestyle. Bit by bit God is changing (recreating) us from inside out. So when we do wrong things and disobey the Spirit within, God forgives us (after repentance) and immediately presses on with His transformation of our lives. So our lifestyle always pleases Jesus, and He "justifies" us before His Father because of our faith in Him. That is, He makes us right day by day, and we live an on-going life in Jesus through the mediation of the Holy Spirit.

God's life within us is always positive, always full of hope, always full of confident expectation, and, because it is accompanied and initiated by the Holy Spirit, invariably succeeds.

Death.

Wouldn't it have been terrible if Adam had run off and eaten the fruit of the Tree of Life? He would still be alive today, as would his children, and the chances are that we wouldn't.

Life can only be given by God, who is the source of all life. Jesus came to bring God's Life. So He says, "Everyone who believes in me will never die." (John 3:16). We will all pass through the transition of separation of our bodies from our souls and spirits, and then what? Those who know Jesus will embrace His Life, in perfection for ever. Those who do not know Jesus will not have Life. Then real death will be theirs for ever (John 5:29). That is the simple truth that the Bible tells us (John 3:36).

See this: Death was the consequence of sin. Law was brought in to curb sin. Now that Jesus has dealt fully with sin of every kind for the Christian, there is no need of law, and death has been removed. Both law and death have become irrelevant in Christ.

What an astonishing thing this Gospel is! What an amazing thing it was that Jesus accomplished on the cross. The principle is there for all mankind. All it needs is for it to be believed and received. In fact, it needs each individual to enter into a personal relationship with Jesus, and all these blessings are granted free, and heaven thrown in for good measure. *"Whenever anyone turns to the Lord, the veil* (of ignorance, blindness and sin) *is taken away."* (2 Cor 3:16).

The Holy Spirit.

It is my personal opinion that the most astonishing thing that Jesus accomplished on the cross was to enable God to send His Holy Spirit down onto all mankind. Why do I think that?

The Holy Spirit has been sent right across the earth. He has access to everyone because all the barriers which separate man from God have been dealt with by the one God-Man Jesus. The Holy Spirit is everywhere all at the same time. He sees all and knows all. He searches the deep things of God (1 Cor 2:10), so He knows the will of God for every individual.

With His presence in our hearts we have been brought right into the heart of the Godhead. Father, Son and Holy Spirit live within us. Jesus said, *"On that day you will realise that I am in my Father, and you are in me, and I am in you."* (John 14:20). In other words, Christians have been integrated into the Godhead, and the presence of the Holy Spirit is not only the guarantee of our inheritance (Eph 1:13-14), and our position in Christ, but the confirmation that God and Christians are One. Jesus is the Head and the church is His Body (Eph 1:22-23). It is absolutely astonishing that humankind has been brought from the depths of degradation, rebellion and separation right up above all other creatures (including angels) and right into the Godhead itself. We are the Bride of Christ as well as the Body of Christ. We are seated with Christ in the heavenly realms at God's right hand (Eph 2:6). *"God demonstrates his own love for us in this: While we were still sinners, Christ died for us."* (Rom 5:8).

The Christian culture is utterly different from the perceptions, the attitudes, the systems and the very fabric of the world in which we live, because it was designed and is being arranged by God Himself. This world and all that is in it is passing away. But the Kingdom of God is growing and lasts for ever (Is 9:6-7).

Righteousness. No one can get into heaven unless they are perfectly righteous. Jesus is the only human being who was, so only He qualifies. *"There is no one righteous, not even one."* (Rom 3:10). But the cross of Jesus has erased all sin in believers, and credited righteousness to them all (Rom 4:5). Then, throughout our lives, the Holy Spirit *imparts* a righteousness to us bit by bit that Christ has initially *imputed*. *"For it is by grace you have been saved, through faith—and this is not from yourselves, it is the gift of God — not by works, so that no one can boast."* (Eph 2:8-9). Only in Jesus does anyone qualify.

Jesus has set mankind free from all his self-indulgent ways (sin), from the system of law that highlighted this sin, and from the consequences of his sin – death. In its place God has given to mankind the Holy Spirit, who brings God and His fullness into every aspect of human life, to transform it for ever into the character and likeness of Jesus. In addition, God describes every believer as perfectly righteous (blameless, faultless), so that all qualify flawlessly for heaven. The whole package is pivoted in and around a personal relationship with Jesus.

That is the Gospel of Jesus Christ, the Good News for all mankind.

The Eternal Covenant.

A covenant is an agreement between two participants. It is different from a contract. A contract is an agreement in law that can be retained, broken or nullified. A covenant is a personal agreement of promise and lasts a lifetime. Marriage is a good example of a covenant.

In the Bible God never made any contracts. But He did make many covenants. All of them were with His people, the Jews, and their ancestors. So He made covenants with Noah, Abraham, Moses, Jeremiah, Ezekiel etc., and His people.

Every covenant has conditions on both sides. *If* you agree to do this, *then* I will agree to do that. Some of God's covenants are still running. The one to Noah, for example, where God said that while the earth remained, seed time and harvest, day and night, summer and winter, cold and heat would never cease, is still working (praise God). Also God's covenant to Abraham and the Jews still remains valid, and has never been rescinded.

Now I have no intention of going into all the covenants that God made with mankind. Instead, I will summarise them thus – God kept His side of the covenants perfectly, but people failed to keep their sides permanently. None of the covenants worked because of the weaknesses in mankind. Mankind was simply unable to be consistent and to keep promises. We can see this very clearly in our own generation by the way that marriage covenants break apart.

So if God was going to make a covenant with mankind that would work, how was He going to accomplish it? The only way He could do it was to do it Himself. God is the only consistent Being in the cosmos on whom He could rely. Angels are failures too.

Now it is very important that we understand the Trinity. One God, three Persons. They are absolutely consistent in their characters, their attitudes, their togethernesses and their unity. They are totally reliable. (Not even the angels are reliable – one third of them defected to satan. And man certainly isn't). But God the Father can utterly rely on His Son and His Spirit.

Thus it was absolutely necessary for Jesus to humble Himself and become a man. If He could live a human life on earth totally consistently, then God the Father could make an everlasting covenant with Him that would work on both sides, and that both could keep eternally.

Mankind is, according to the Bible, God's ultimate creation. Therefore God made Jesus a man, not an animal or an angel. Jesus was tempted in all points like we are, but without sin (Heb 4). Therefore God was completely satisfied with Jesus' obedience while He was on earth, and thereby was enabled to make an everlasting covenant with Him.

What is that covenant? It is that every human being who wished to join God in heaven at the end of their lives would have to surrender their lives to Jesus during their lifetime. Only "In Christ" can anyone qualify for heaven. That must be obvious – every other human being on earth has lived a selfish, ungodly life on most days in their lives. But if any person runs to Jesus and comes under His umbrella, he becomes a participant in the eternal covenant that God made with His Son. Jesus told us how that would work – anyone whom He, Jesus, loved and forgave would be approved and accepted by His Father. (John 14:23-24).

In addition, Jesus would send the Holy Spirit to indwell that individual, so that the ability to please God would be gifted to that person inside. Thus Jesus on one hand and the Holy Spirit on the other would enable that person to qualify for heaven. Only God is perfectly and consistently reliable. God outside us and God inside us enable that covenant to work perfectly.

So when a person surrenders their lives to Jesus for Him to direct, the whole Trinity comes to live inside them. That is the only way in which a human being can possibly enter God's heaven. God has to do it in them.

But what about sin? There is no human being on earth who does not occasionally fall into the traps of temptation, and follow the lusts of their hearts.

Sin for someone in Christ is forgiven instantly on repentance. That is absolutely fabulous. What a provision! It is forgiven because Jesus died in the place of every Christian, taking both their sin and their punishment on His shoulders. So we are cleansed every day of our new lives by the forgiveness of Jesus and we are directed daily towards righteousness by the indwelling Holy Spirit. God has perfected for ever mankind's return to a life of eternal significance by doing all the hard work Himself. That is grace and mercy *par excellence.*

Through all the developing covenants that God has had with mankind, none of which worked perfectly, this last one is perfect. No consideration has been left out. It is a covenant that works perfectly for every single human being that lives or will ever live on earth. It has no rivals. Anyone, from the youngest to the oldest, from the most ignorant to the most intelligent, from the isolated peasant to the most privileged and most important world leader can access the glory and forgiveness of God and participate in the eternal new world of the new heavens and earth. There is no other way that this can be accomplished in the cosmos. Jesus is the only way.

This covenant is an Eternal Covenant. THE Eternal Covenant. It works perfectly every time, and throughout the ages of earth.

"In the same way, after supper he took the cup, saying, This cup is the new covenant in my blood; do this, whenever you drink it, in remembrance of me." (1 Cor 11:25).

"May the God of peace, who through the blood of the eternal covenant brought back from the dead our Lord Jesus, that great Shepherd of the sheep, equip you with everything good for doing his will, and may he work in us what is pleasing to him, through Jesus Christ, to whom be glory for ever and ever. Amen." (Heb 13:20-21).

Therefore, when believers in Jesus drink the communion cup, we do so remembering that it is the blood of the Eternal Covenant made between God and Jesus, and in which we are totally undeserving participants. We have been done to by the God of all Grace. Be thankful and humbly grateful for ever.

Characteristics of the Holy Spirit.

It is my personal opinion that the most astonishing thing that Jesus accomplished on the cross was to enable God to send His Holy Spirit down onto all mankind. Why do I think that?

Before Jesus came, the Holy Spirit was given a very limited access to individuals. Only a few experienced His presence. That was because their lives were still sinful, and God cannot live with anyone who is still self-determining – God's will and man's will are mutually irreconcilable. So the Holy Spirit was only sent to a very few special people for special occasions.

But now the Holy Spirit has been sent right across the earth. He has access to everyone because all the barriers which separate man from God have been dealt with by the one God-Man Jesus. The Holy Spirit is everywhere all at the same time. He sees all and knows all. He searches the deep things of God (1 Cor 2:10), so He knows the will of God for every individual.

Now see some other things that the release of the Holy Spirit implies.

With His presence in our hearts we have been brought right into the heart of the Godhead. Father, Son and Holy Spirit live within us. Jesus said, *"On that day you will realise that I am in my Father, and you are in me, and I am in you."* (John 14:20). In other words, Christians have been integrated into the Godhead, and the presence of the Holy Spirit is not only the guarantee of our inheritance (Eph 1:13-14), and our position in Christ, but the confirmation that God and Christians are One. Jesus is the Head and the church is His Body (Eph 1:22-23). It is absolutely astonishing that humankind has been brought from the depths of degradation, rebellion and separation right up above all other creatures (including angels) and right into the Godhead itself. We are the Bride of Christ as well as the Body of Christ. We are seated with Christ in the heavenly realms at God's right hand (Eph 2:6). *"God demonstrates his own love for us in this: While we were still sinners, Christ died for us."* (Rom 5:8).

See this also. God has begun to restore the whole earth to His original intention. He has dealt a mortal blow to the whole fabric of man-made institutions. The whole world system has been weighed in the balances and found wanting, its cultures and ways of living have been declared empty, useless and dead. They will all be replaced by God's system. God, who is in everything and through everything, runs this whole universe by the Trinity's own power and infinite ability, but by grace, kindness, wisdom and goodness. God also knows (and has told us in the Bible) that the vast majority of humankind will not accept the redemption and restoration that He has freely provided (Matt 7:13-14). Therefore they will press on in their self-centred ways and self-destruct the whole world.

So how is God going to restore His ways to the world?

He is choosing individuals, from among the people, who love Him back and will do His will. He brings them closer to Himself throughout their lifetime, and then removes them, preserving them for later. At the Second Coming of Jesus God will give to each of them a new resurrection body that is eternal. This body will be like Jesus' resurrection body and will be far better than Adam's original super body. These people will reign with Jesus over the earth for a thousand years, and then with Him over a new heaven and a new earth and over the whole universe on into the far distant future – as the Bride of Christ. God has seen that it is impossible for Christians to restore God's original intention for the earth while there are still self-determined people running it. So Jesus will deal with all of them when He returns in power and great glory. Only He can do it.

But do you see the future that God has in mind for us? He is going to sweep away this beautiful earth and cosmos and replace it with a more beautiful one over which the Bride of Christ will reign with Him for ever. So He has started small. He talks to individuals and reveals Himself to them so that they can choose Him instead of themselves. When they choose Jesus, he sends them the Holy Spirit to be their guide and guard for ever. Again and again the New Testament tells us that it is the Holy Spirit who is God within us, and is the key to knowing whether we have the real thing or just a human counterfeit.

Let's see what the Bible says about how the Holy Spirit works within us.

We are born into the spiritual family of God by the Spirit (John 3:6). We live by the Spirit (Rom 8:5). We walk in the Spirit (Gal 5:16). We pray in the Spirit (1 Cor 14:15). We speak in the Spirit (1 Cor 2:13). We worship in the Spirit (John 4:23-24). We sing in the Spirit (1 Cor 14:15). We have the mind of the Spirit (Rom 8:6). We are led by the Spirit, *"for all who are led by the Spirit are sons of God"* (Rom 8:14). The Spirit guides us (John 16:13). The Spirit is our strength (Acts 1:8). He is the Spirit of wisdom (Eph 1:17), the Spirit of truth (John 16:13), the Spirit of revelation (Eph 1:17). Through the Spirit we overcome fleshly desires (Gal 5:16). We cast out demon spirits by the Spirit of God (Matt 12:28). The Spirit helps us in our weaknesses (Rom 8:26). We have access into God by the Spirit (Eph 2:18). We are being renewed in the spirit of our minds (Rom 12:2). God has not given us a spirit of fear, but of love, power and self-control (2 Tim 1:7). The Spirit sanctifies us (makes us more holy) (2 Thess 2:13). If we live by the Spirit we are delivered from the supervision (and bondage) of man's law (Gal 3:25). We develop the fruit of the Spirit in our natures (love, joy, peace, patience, kindness, goodness, faithfulness, gentleness and self-control) (Gal 5:22-23). The Spirit is the guarantee of our inheritance (Eph 1:13-14). He is exactly like Jesus (John 16:13-15), who will never abandon or forsake us (Matt 28:20, John 14:18). The Spirit has power (Acts 1:8). The Spirit talks to us (1 Cor 2:11-12). He is the Spirit of holiness (Rom 1:4). The Spirit cleans us up (2 Cor 7:1). He is the Spirit of meekness and humility (Phil 2:1-4). There are also supernatural gifts from the Holy Spirit that enhance our ministries (1 Cor 12:7-11).

At the same time, the Holy Spirit brings Jesus into our hearts. He is our Shepherd, our Guide, our Guard, and the Alpha and Omega – the whole purpose of living, the beginning, the middle and the end of all things for us. He is our Husband, our friend, our lover and our greatest prize. If we have got Jesus, we've got everything. If we don't have Jesus, we've got nothing. The Holy Spirit is both the sign and seal inside us (Eph 1:14) that all things are ours through Jesus, for ever (1 Cor 3:21-23). Jesus is the eternal Yes (12 Cor 1:18-20), the answer to every prayer, every perception and every dream of goodness. All things are possible in Jesus (Matt 19:26, Mark 10:27). The works that He did on earth are also ours to do, and even greater works than His because He has gone to the Father (John 14:12).

The Christian culture is utterly different from the perceptions, the attitudes, the systems and the very fabric of the world in which we live, because it was designed and is being arranged by God Himself. This world and all that is in it is passing away. But the Kingdom of God is growing and lasts for ever:

"For to us a child is born, to us a son is given, and the government will be on his shoulders. And he will be called Wonderful Counsellor, Mighty God, Everlasting Father, Prince of Peace. Of the increase of his government and peace there will be no end. He will reign on David's throne and over his kingdom, establishing and upholding it with justice and righteousness from that time on and forever. The zeal of the Lord Almighty will accomplish this." (Is 9:6-7).

Walking in the Spirit.

The idea of "Walking in the Spirit" is the new and living way that Jesus has opened up for all mankind. If we live this way we live a perfect life, in full harmony and fellowship with God, and please Him in everything we are and do. We also please other people. So how does this work? *How* do we walk in the Spirit? (This is the same chapter deliberately repeated from Book 2).

First let me summarise the basics for you. Then I will take you through one of my days to show it working. I will put the scriptures in brackets for you to look up for yourselves if you wish. Generally it would make this chapter far too long for me to quote them all on paper.

Jesus has been given all authority in heaven and earth (Matt 28:18). All that God the Father has He has given to Jesus (John 16:15), and the Holy Spirit will take what belongs to Jesus and will give it to us (John 16:15). Jesus said that He would never leave us or abandon us (Matt 28:20), and that He would come to those who love Him but not to those who do not (John 14:16-19). The Holy Spirit, drawing from Jesus' Sovereign knowledge, will teach us *all* things (John 14:26); that we might know (Col 2:3).

So, we have the whole Trinity living inside us to guide and direct us in everything we do so that we are enabled to please God in every second of our lives.

But God has not taken our wills away from us. So, although the Holy Spirit is actually directing us in everything we do, we can still choose not to do it. Indeed, we have even to choose to obey His promptings because none of them come with absolute certainty.

For those moments when we have no certain knowledge of whether the Spirit is prompting us or not, Jesus has left us His peace as the guide that what we are doing is pleasing to God. *"Let the peace of Christ rule in your hearts…"* (Col 3:15). *"Peace I leave with you; my peace I give you. I do not give to you as the world gives. Do not let your hearts be troubled and do not be afraid."* (John 14:27). (John 14:27).

So, first then, a word about peace. There are two kinds – external and internal. External peace is the ceasing of aggravation on the outside of us (and actually forms the subject of the majority of our prayers). Internal peace is that which only Jesus can give us, and is governed by being in His will, knowing that He is in control of all things, and that He will work out everything gently, perfectly and satisfactorily. Consequently, don't ever get anxious and don't ever get fearful – the two major things that will destroy our internal peace (as Jesus pointed out in the scripture above).

In this world we will have aggravation – or tribulation as Jesus put it (John 16:33KJV). It is satan's particular job and expertise to bring us trouble at any and every point in our earthly lives. We do not wrestle against flesh and blood (people) but against the spiritual forces of evil in the heavenly realms (Eph 6:12).

Mostly we focus our praying on eliminating the *external* trouble. But we would often do better to pray for Jesus' *internal* peace to prevail in the hearts of those for whom we pray. If they can ride the hassle by leaning on Jesus' peace, they will gain victory over the hassle. Satan hates people retaining their faith in Jesus, and the glory that accompanies the peace pushes satan away (2 Cor 3:18, 4:4-6). The Holy Spirit will guide us into Jesus' peace, and will remind us of every promise of God's that applies to our Now situation (John 14:26, 2 Peter 1:4), because *"His divine power has given us everything we need for life and godliness through our knowledge of him who called us by his own glory and goodness."* (2 Peter 1:3).

So, the Holy Spirit will direct us in everything we do, whether practical, spiritual, secular, in our behaviour, or in our heart's attitudes and at all times will bring us Jesus' peace. *"Do not be anxious about anything, but in everything by prayer and petition, with thanksgiving, present your requests to God. And the peace of God, which transcends all understanding, will guard your hearts and your minds in Christ Jesus."* (Phil 4:6-7).

So, *where* does the Holy Spirit guide us best? In our ordinary domestic lives. In the home and at our place of work. Remember that Jesus learned how to obey God, grow in wisdom and develop His relationship with His Father by living 30 years in an ordinary home doing ordinary things. The ordinary is God's school. You will never be the channel for God to do *extraordinary* things through you if first of all you don't allow Him to do things through you. Jesus never did one miracle in 30 years; He honed the skill of hearing His Father's voice first and doing only what God said to Him. That took 30 years – the majority of His earthly life. He was then ready and perfected to be the channel for God to do miracles and teaching through Him, only because He could now hear God's internal instructions very clearly and concerning every circumstance.

So, does *how* the Holy Spirit guide us? It's by thoughts in our minds. And it is particularly in the little things. Human beings are built such that all their actions are first preceded by thinking and deciding. I have come to the conclusion that whether you are male or female, it works the same. You think something, debate it inside, and then decide whether to do it or not to do it.

So it is in the mind where God directs us. He has total access to our minds.

He "pops" a thought into the mind.

We are so used to "getting" thoughts that we take it for granted that they all come from us. Because they appear spontaneously in our minds, we have always naturally assumed that they originate from us. But very few do.

For instance, all temptation starts as a thought in the mind. And temptation certainly does not originate from us. It hits us inside but does not belong to us. It is always geared to our vulnerabilities, weaknesses and our lusts, but it begins with satan and/or his hairy bunch of demons. They also have open access to our minds.

So does God. Every thought of goodness, kindness, generosity etc., originates in God, and *He* puts those kinds of thoughts into our minds (James 1:17).

We cannot identify either God's or satan's thoughts inside our minds. They just come in as "things" – inanimate thoughts. But we *listen* to satan's thoughts far easier than God's because they are tuned to our fleshly desires. We don't "want" to do God's thoughts because they don't particularly contain pleasure. But they will all be actions of goodness and all require obedience. We must *choose* to do good rather than evil. The good thoughts from God come into our minds at any time but *always* during temptation to enable us to avoid it and choose goodness (1 Cor 10:13).

Now think of this: if God told us that it was He who was speaking, there would be no room for faith. We would walk by knowledge, not by faith, and the scripture says that we walk by faith not by sight (2 Cor 5:7). In order that we should walk by faith, God has to inject uncertainty into the thoughts He places in our minds. So none of them come with any inkling that they are from the Holy Spirit, who will *"teach us all things"* and guide us in everything we do. They always come in as suggestions. Not commands.

Consequently, it leaves the choice of what we do up to us. God puts the prompting into our minds, and we either select or deselect the thought by our wills, in our hearts. In this way, every one of us is fully accountable for deciding and doing the actions we take (and consequently judgement in the final great assizes in heaven will be perfectly fair). The same is true of temptation. Satan is not allowed to *cause* us to sin. He puts the temptations into our minds and we do the tempted thing or not through our own decisions. The Great Judgement at the end of time is not just about when we yielded to temptation and sinned, but for when we decided to obey God's suggestions or not concerning good things. Even the things God puts into our minds need to be engaged with faith (that is, believing that *He* has put that thought into our minds). Truly we are terminally fallen creatures, and none of us will survive the Judgement without the reconciliation and forgiveness of Jesus.

So now let me try to tell you how this works by giving you a selection of things that happened to me in one day.

The background to this day is that, two weeks previously, Eileen had slipped and fallen in the street, had broken her hip bone and a rib bone, had bruised her left side in many other places, and was deposited in various hospitals. It was a disaster – the kind of external aggravation that I talked about earlier. The first victory I got was my internal peace; I refused to be anxious, worried or fearful about this accident.

Eileen has run our house. She does the cooking, cleaning, laundry and gardening. I repair the house and help Eileen when she asks me, and, of course, I have a job of work to do in Nicaragua. But that division has meant that I have been singularly ignorant of domestic affairs and apparatus. So the day which I describe is a very good example as it falls within the category of my total ignorance.

For clarity, I will try to differentiate between my thoughts and God's thoughts within my mind.

So, after breakfast, what do I do next? There's the mail to read, the washing up to do, the emails to read and reply to, cat to feed, vacuuming to do, dishwasher to empty, shopping to do, laundry to wash, ironing to do, Exeter to travel to to collect printing, and kit to collect for Eileen for me to take to hospital.

In came the thought "One thing at a time." That thought was from God –

thank you Lord. I have often lost my internal peace by worry or hurry trying to do everything all at once, and have made other people angry or brought them into dis-peace by hassling them by pushing them to move faster than they are used to. So I had to come into peace over the commitments for today, and that came by determining to do one thing only at a time and obeying the Lord. So which to do first?

"Feed the cat." OK. (God, but not acknowledged by me as such, so not an action of faith). Done.

"Do the emails." OK Lord. (God, and acknowledged in faith). "Even though you have many things to do, respond to the emails and get them out of the way." OK Lord. (God, and done in faith). But satan is here to try to make me answer the emails quickly and without thought – "there's so much to be done so push on and skip quickly over them. Some you can leave out altogether." This conflicted with the Lord's thoughts. Reject it and come into God's peace on every email.

Having done them "Put the dirty laundry in the washing machine." God – but not acknowledged as such by me, but now working in the Lord's peace. So I do God's will in peace, but the choice to do it was not an act of faith.

"Do the washing up." That was from God. This I do not want to do. There are too many other important things that need doing to take valuable time out to do that. So I come into conflict with the Lord. I debate it, but then move reluctantly in faith that it was God's suggestion and do the washing up. (I am far more like the Son in Jesus' parable who said No and did it, rather than the Son who said Yes and did not do it (Matt 21:28-31)). In addition, I have learned the hard way that the Lord knows the whole future, so if He suggests that I do the washing up now, it clearly indicates that He is saving me aggravation in the future. I will never know what that aggravation might be if I do God's will straight away. Do I *really* want to know what He is saving me from? So I do the washing up.

"Sort out the mail". I just followed that thought without considering whether it was from the Lord or not. I just did it. So – not an act of faith. And *"Everything that does not come from faith is sin."* (Rom 14:23b). (Nasty verse, that).

"Go to Exeter. Remember to take the cheque book for the printing and the broken tent poles to change." OK Lord. I got that one in faith.

Surprisingly enough, I was able to leave for Exeter quite early. Something else I have found is that if I am walking by God's Spirit and in God's peace, everything takes far shorter time and is done far more effectively than when I am in hurry-mode and pushing everything in my own strength. *"Not by might, nor by power, but by my Spirit, says the Lord."* (Zech 4:6). In the car, travelling slower and in God's peace gets me there quicker and faster than driving tensed up like a Formula One driver. Don't ask me how that works – it just does. Check it out for yourself.

The printing was collected OK (and I was glad for the reminder to take the cheque book along), and on the way into Exeter I asked the Lord for a car parking space. I now do this on every journey. In 40 years I have had only one occasion when there was no space made available by the Lord. "Go to the covered car park," came the thought. I replied "That is not my normal car park, and it's further away than my usual one. Why should I go there?" Silence. So I then spent the next few minutes arguing with the Lord in my mind as to why I should go there and not to my normal one. But He gave me no reply. God does not argue or discuss – He only tells. So, very reluctantly, and discarding my need for a logical reason, I went to the covered car park. If God says that that is the best place for me to park, then He clearly has very good reasons why I should go there and not anywhere else. So that became an act of faith even though it was done with a bad attitude.

I always have a tune running around my mind, and I try to keep those melodies heavenly. So as I walked down the street, taking note of everyone just in case I could do them a random act of kindness, I hummed *I will sing of Your love for ever ...* Then in the High Street I met Tracey. She is a school teacher in the school of which I am a Governor, and she was there with her husband (it was school summer holidays). I gave her a hug and she asked where I was going. To change the poles of the tent, one of which had broken. She had just come from that part of town and said that there were about four shops there which I could try. I only knew of one, so I thanked her. Indeed, that was a divine appointment (even though she would not have known that). The first tent-pole shop I came across had the item I wanted and it cost only a little. So this thought popped into my mind: "That's what happens when you walk in the Lord's peace and are looking for His will at every moment in time." That was definitely a thought from the Lord, so I thanked Him and returned to the car.

On the way home I encountered red traffic lights. Now I had learned as a very young Christian to give thanks in all things (I Thess 5:18, Eph 5:20), and that that certainly included red traffic lights. So I smiled at most and laughed at the last few. At one of them I broke off a square of chocolate to chew. The thought for that definitely did not come from the Lord, but I was driving in His peace, so it was clear that He did not disapprove. After all, He has given us all things richly to enjoy, so I richly enjoyed a bit of chocolate (1 Tim 6:17).

On the way home, now humming *He is able to do exceeding abundantly more than we ask or think …*, it turned foggy with low cloud on the top of the hills. "Turn on your lights." Indeed, thank you Lord. BE SEEN. It's one of the best rules in the Highway Code to turn on dipped headlights in inclement weather. So as I drove on, I got increasingly cross with other passing drivers who did not have their headlights on or who only had parking lights on. I guess I've got a thing about it. So I flashed them as I went past, just to remind them of the law. At which point I got entangled again with the Lord. Getting cross about something I can do nothing about (the ignorance and disobedience of other drivers) is stupid, is far from grace, and loses my internal peace. I felt the Lord's frown. He reminded me that *"Sin shall not be your master, because you are not under law, but under grace."* (Rom 6:14). Leave all these other drivers with the Lord. It is His responsibility to remind them of the right thing to do, not mine. And He can put that thought into their minds just as easily as He put it into mine. So I prayed for them instead of getting cross with them. But it certainly was hard to change the way I felt about them.

I think that's enough of the detail. The Lord is intensely interested in every little detail of our lives, and is involved at every point. He not only knows more about our own past than we can ever remember, but He has the only perfect handle on circumstances in the future to guide us right at this moment. He is involved from the moment we wake up to the moment we drop to sleep, and is making suggestions all the time so that we can live our lives in perfect harmony with Him, walking by faith in the thoughts He puts into our minds moment by moment.

You will have noticed that my reactions to the Lord's thoughts in my mind were varied – ignore them, debate them, reject them, do them without engaging faith, acknowledge them with faith, or discard them and do my own thing. I'm certain that my varied reactions will be exactly in tune with yours. God is looking for direct acknowledgement and straight obedience from all of us for every one of His thoughts. This is *The* way He guides us.

Jesus has total access to both our minds and our situations. He is involved, for example, in our toilet – what we do in there and when we should buy more soap, toothpaste, toilet rolls, razor blades, deodorant etc., and will remind us of all these things when we forget them. After all, Jesus used toilet "stuff" as illustrations five times in the Gospels.

He knows each of us as individuals, and also knows whether we are fussy or messy home makers. And He will prompt us appropriate to our characters and to the way we want to live. So, He will not force us to be tidy or fussy home makers if our character is to be less tidy and more comfortable. He directs us *inside* our individuality. We should not do things in the home "because they need to be done." We do them at the prompting of the Holy Spirit, and live in God's peace. If something cannot be done today, then He will remind us tomorrow. There is no reason why anyone should be in stress in regard to the home or the place of work.

Some people (including my Eileen) say that this level of involvement by God in the home is nonsense. Any housewife will know what is to be done. It is common sense based on daily experience. But they are wrong. Many (most?) housewives get very stressed in their homes about routine domestic affairs. If only they recognised the Lord promptings and His Sovereignty, they would live in His peace and simply do what He says at the time He put the thought in their minds.

Most Christian men do not communicate with God in their work places. They use the world's training to do their jobs, learning more of the world's ways as they go along. But Jesus is Lord of every work place. He knows more about economy, technology, management, and work skills – whether by hand or by brain – than any other human being in the universe. How can a Christian man glorify God in his workplace unless he hears and *listens* to the Lord's internal promptings in his mind and does them? The man who built his house on the rock was the man who *heard* Jesus' words and *did* them. (Matt 7:24-27).

Let me illustrate this with letter writing. I have often got the prompting to write a letter to someone. Sometimes, for many reasons, I didn't. But the Holy Spirit has kept nudging me. In the end, sometimes after weeks of delay, I write it and post it. Then back comes the reply that my letter was exactly on time, and solved the problem that was a bother at that moment. So, the Holy Spirit knows the future perfectly. So He plans ahead and nudges and nudges until He knows I'm going to do it. He also knows the difficulties of the person I am writing to, and His nudging blends perfectly with the problem. He knows my laziness, my procrastination, my disobedience, my bad choices, and plans them all into His promptings. He has often had to plan me six months ahead in this.

It is in the *normal routine things* that God is easiest to be found. If we do not or cannot recognise His inputs there, we will never find His inputs for the big things. When asked when and how the Lord last spoke to us, most of us go for the special occasions: "Last year when ..." How dull it is to say "A couple of minutes ago, He ..." Are we trying to impress man or glorify God? How silly to ignore His little daily inputs waiting for the big ones. Remember again that Jesus waited 30 years in peace for His calling into Ministry. He was in no hurry – everything was under His Father's control, and His Father needed to teach Him more about His Sovereignty in ordinary living so that He would be fully equipped for His Ministry. If we are familiar with the way the Holy Spirit prompts us in our homes and work places, the big callings will be no different in style.

Do a Bible study on the Holy Spirit. You will find every aspect of human life covered by His inputs. Then put it into practice throughout your days, and watch what wonderful things God can do through you - even in your homes or work places. And live in God's internal peace – it is The *sign* that you are walking in His will.

"So I say, live by the Spirit, and you will not gratify the desires of the sinful nature. For the sinful nature desires what is contrary to the Spirit, and the Spirit what is contrary to the sinful nature. They are in conflict with each other, so that you are not to do whatever you want. But if you are led by the Spirit you are not under law." (Gal 5:16-18).

Martin Luther wrote: "Grant the Holy Spirit the honour of being more learned than you."

Redemption

Take care, reader! If you dare to read on you could come across many things that will surprise and challenge you.

So, following my own convention, let's start with the known and go to the unknown, with the simple and go on to the spiritual.

The word redemption is in common use, and simply means to buy back. Pawnbrokers use it a lot. You hand your precious watch in to them to obtain cash, and, later, after your pay packet has come in, you "redeem" your watch back again.

The word is used frequently in the New Testament, and is invariably used for Jesus' redemption. It's a metaphor from the pawnbroker. Jesus' death on the cross has paid the price of man's rebellion, and has enabled God the Father to "buy back" human beings from the separation of death. When you hand your watch in to the pawnbroker, you become separated from it. To redeem it is to restore your close relationship with it. That is the metaphor of heaven. Only in God is there life and oneness. Those who are not in God are only in death. That is because they are separated from Him. They are actually in the hands of satan, follow his lead, because they are utterly self-orientated. Self-centredness is *The* characteristic of satan. We have placed ourselves in the place that God should have in our lives. This, as you would know, is called sin, and is the root of man's separation from God. "Sin" and "Death" are synonyms, both symptoms of separation from the God who is the Universe. No one can be self-centred and Christ-centred at the same time.

What the cross of Jesus enabled God to do was to pay the price of redemption – enabling Him to bring every human being who wants to back into reconciliation with Him. From separation to conciliation.

Now a little word as to why this should be important. In existence there are only two "things", only two places to live, only two possibilities. There is either God or "me". I am either living in God or living in myself. Outside of me (that is, my self-centred being) there is only God. God the Trinity is the beginning, middle and end of all existence. Without Them there would not be anything in existence at all. Inside my heart and soul, I either live with me in its centre or God in its centre. If I live with myself in the centre, I share it with no one else in the universe – except satan. But all he can do is to increase my isolation, because he is the source of all independence and self-centredness. I am alone, and ever more alone with satan.

But if I surrender myself to God through Jesus I share the rest of my existence both with Him and therefore with every other human being who has also surrendered their lives to Jesus, and with the rest of creation. In that state I would never be lonely again, never alone again.

This is not all that obvious while we are here on earth, because we share life on earth on the outside with other people. But the reality of our own hearts is still true – we are either alone with no one else, or with Jesus and, through Him, with everyone else and with the rest of the cosmos. There is no middle ground. No one else can live inside me – not like Jesus can. He brings companionship and reconciliation with the cosmos.

God calls self-orientation death, and you can see why. When our body dies and our souls are separated from them, we will have left *everything* of earth behind and we are into the reality of the universe. And we are either totally alone for the rest of eternity, or totally reconciled to God, to His heavenly host and to His creation for eternity. If we have not been redeemed, or reconciled, we are in terrible trouble. There is no alternative – it's either me alone or the God of Jesus. There is no one and nothing else.

This earth needed redeeming. Adam's choice in Eden to go his own way rather than God's brought death to the whole of his successors – to all mankind. Self-centredness of heart is integrated with separation from God and death to human bodies. It also brought death to the earth and the cosmos. All plants and animals die, as do all our building works, as do the stars. The scientists call it entropy – everything decaying to chaos. We live in a world of continuous death.

What Christians call redemption was very costly and very complex. None of us had any idea just how disastrous our rebellion was to the whole future of the universe. God's plan extends far beyond the history of this earth. He has plans for a new heaven and a new earth that far exceed the imagination of any man, and are eternal. But without man to manage it with Him, those plans would come to nothing. If all humans remained in death, who would administer God's universe for Him and with Him? His plan was that man should, and He had planned no alternative. Angels were not good enough. So the death of Jesus was crucial and central to the whole of the future – both creation's future and ours. God paid the ultimate price to buy us back from the isolation and separation of death. Jesus redeemed us. "I'll never know how much it cost to see my sins upon that cross."

Jesus is the Redeemer. There is no one else. No other religion has a redeemer that works. Hinduism has, at the last count, somewhere near 330,000 gods, and some are supposed to redeem. But all they are doing is trying to copy Jesus. If Hindus find something lacking in their religion, they invent another god. But Jesus is *God's* Redeemer. That's why He works perfectly every time.

Jesus' redemption is through relationships. His redemption brings reconciliation with Father God. If we surrender our rebellion and our self determination, and allow Jesus to be Lord over our lives, we become friends of God. From the moment of our repentance and capitulation, we are centred for ever around God in a personal relationship on the inside. We are reconciled with heaven, reconciled with creation, reconciled with every other human being and reconciled with ourselves. We start to live in peace. We are isolated no longer. We join an innumerable company of people and creatures who will live for ever in joy. That's God's redemption.

This is not always that obvious on earth, but when our body dies, then it becomes glaringly obvious. There we will know are we are now fully known (1 Cor 13:12).

So, starting at the point of redemption, what happens? Jesus begins with us as individuals. Our entrance into God's heaven is only the beginning. There are vast tracts of selfishness that are displeasing to God still left in our lives.

One by one, Jesus brings before us some aspect of our lives that is not fit for heaven or not pleasing to Him. He is so gentle in His exposing of these things. But listen to the word "redeem". Jesus exposes what is wrong and, as we surrender it to Him, He redeems it. That is, He kills the bad and transforms it into something beautiful and good – He "buys back" our heart attitude from the death attitude that has enslaved it (Rom 6:18). There are certain things that cannot be transformed, and those He rids us of for ever. But He does not leave it there – He replaces the vacuum left by the disappearance of the bad thing with some good attitude or quality that comes from Him. Jesus is reconstructing every human being who surrenders to Him into God's own likeness of perfection (Eph 4:24). The whole of our days are an adventure of transformation – of restoration - from inside out.

That's the measure of redemption that God in Jesus does *to* us.

But that is not the end. Jesus also does things *through* us.

In John 15 Jesus gave us a lovely metaphor of the vine. He is the true vine. His Father is the vine-dresser or gardener. We are the branches. The purpose of a vine is to produce grapes. That can only happen if the branch remains in the vine. So obvious. The Gardener prunes the branches so that they can produce grapes, more grapes and many grapes. Any fruitless branch that is cut off withers and dies, and is thrown into the fire. Let's not talk about them – let's talk about the good branches. Jesus said, *"Without me you can do nothing."* (John 15:5).

But *with* Him, what is happening? What is the nature of the grapes that come from His vine through His pruned branches? I tell you, it's not just being nice guys, good people, or happy folks. The impact of the metaphor is not what we *are* so much as what we *do*. The grapes represent acts of God that come through us. The grapes are not any old grapes. They are *God's* grapes.

So what are they?

They are all acts of redemption, restoration and reconciliation.

Every act of God to mankind is redemptive and reconciliatory. That is because the whole of earth – physical, animal and human, needs redeeming. Everything is dead and separated from God, and needs redemption and reconciliation. He is using Christians as His route for divine redemption.

God's wonderful initiative in redemption enabled Christians to be channels of restoration. We restore people to their designed relationship with God through Jesus, and we restore the earth from chaos to the order and beauty of the design intention. All sorts of people are doing the latter – but the Christian has a divine element incorporated within them that restores according to God's redemption. That is, we bring Life to it, not just order and justice.

So let us look at some of those details.

Prayer. My Bible says that when I ask anything in line with God's will, I will get what I ask for (1 John 5:14-15). How do I know I am asking in accordance with His will? Well, if I first of all ask God the Holy Spirit what I should pray for and how I should pray, then the answer He gives me is always in accordance with God's will. That prayer is always answered "Yes". Now see this - those prayers are always redemptive. They always work. They always bring healing or wholeness – a change in the person's life that releases God's perfect will and redemption into their lives. So many of our prayers are hit and miss. We are seldom sure whether they will work, but we hope so. That is *not* God's way of praying. God's ways of prayer really make big inroads into other people's lives and situations. God's kind of prayer changes things very effectively. His prayers are always redemptive. Come into faith in relation to this, and make all your prayers powerful and transformational. *Believe* it. Christians are channels of God's redemption, restoration and reconciliation through Jesus.

Words. I have pointed out elsewhere that God only operates by speaking. So all His inputs into our minds are spoken personally by Him. That has enormous implications. It means that everything He says to us is redemptive. So when we speak in accordance with the prompting of the Holy Spirit, we are operating like God Himself, and our words bring Life (see 1 Thess 2:13). Indeed, they bring redemption and reconciliation. All Jesus' words on earth brought Life and redemption. They still do as we read them in the Gospels. He is transforming us to be like Himself, like God. So He is teaching us to check out our words with Him before we speak them so that they become redemptive too. Paul told us how to do this: the significant passage is 1 Cor 2:9–16. Note particularly verse 13: *"This is what we speak, not in words taught us by human wisdom but in words taught by the Spirit, expressing spiritual truths in spiritual words."* I don't know if you are anything like me: most of the things I say are surface, thoughtless, puerile, stupid and are designed to impress the listeners. They so often go badly wrong, and I have so frequently said things that hurt, are unhelpful or are idiotic. I often get rebuked by the Lord through Jesus' words in my Bible: *"But I tell you that men will have to give account on the day of judgement for every careless word they have spoken. For by your words you will be acquitted, and by your words you will be condemned."* (Matt 12:36-37). Very slowly and very patiently the Lord is trying to control my tongue. I am learning to keep silent much more than I ever did. And I'm trying to make my words be a repetition of the words the Holy Spirit is prompting inside my mind, so that they can bring Life and redemption. It worked like that the other day: I was standing behind a man trying to pay for his car parking. He couldn't fathom the machine and said, "Oh Christ." I said quietly to him from behind, "How wonderful to meet someone else who prays." He turned and laughed; it was a redemptive word that I gave him, because he knew exactly what he had said and why, and exactly what I was saying.

Deeds. Again, I have written elsewhere that the new life in Jesus comes about by walking in the Spirit. The Holy Spirit prompts us in the tiny little things of life – what we should do next. This is especially true domestically in our homes, in the street or work places. It so happens that every little prompting from God is perfect in every respect. It is the right thing to do at every moment in time. It stops the hassle later on from happening that will certainly happen if we fail to act on His prompting. In other words, it's redemptive. "Do the washing up now", coming from the Holy Spirit, is redemptive. It foresees hassle in the future, clears the mess of this moment, and releases time in the future for the important thing of that moment. The metaphor of the vine says that if we abide in Jesus, and His words abide in us, we produce divine grapes, all of which are redemptive. So the more we listen to the Holy Spirit's prompting and do what He tells us when He tells us to do it, we live a life of redemption. We not only live in peace inside, we *bring* peace into every situation we are in. Redemption is not just *in* us, but *through* us – as I pointed out earlier. *"Blessed are the peacemakers, for they will be called sons of God."* (Matt 5:9). All Christian ministries are redemptive: preaching, teaching, counselling, building, helping etc. So should all Christians' lives be.

Eph 5:16 (KJV) tells us to *"Redeem the time, for the days are evil."* Adam's choice in Eden not only brought death to mankind, death to all animal and vegetable life, death to all Nature, death to the cosmos, but death to time itself. Time, by nature, is death and brings death. This is part of the entropy that scientists tell us is the universal characteristic of all creation. Time brings death to all of nature. Christians are the catalyst that slows down this death and even reverses it. Indeed, they are the only catalyst. We do our little bits of redeeming all over the earth until Jesus returns and redeems everything back to God.Only in God is there Life. Christians are the agents of God on earth, the mediators of Divine Life. So as we seek the Lord's face and do His will daily, we buy back every action and word in time so that it creates Life and restoration in everything we do and say. We are the mediators of the New Covenant that God has with His creation, and also with time as well.

And still I have not finished. There is one other thing I need to point out. If we are walking with the Lord in this way and are bringing redemption fruitfulness as we walk, pray, talk and act, we become redeemers ourselves. Every person or family to whom we minister the Lord's Life of redemption and reconciliation see us as their "saviour". We are to them Jesus in a human form. They regard us as the person who has brought peace and reconciliation into their lives. Consider your Pastor or Church leader – someone who brings God's word and counsel faithfully to you. We hang on their words. We gain spiritual insight and wisdom through their leadership, preaching and teaching. They are a channel of Jesus' redemption, and are themselves redeemers to us.

They know that they are simply channels of God's grace and reconciliation. But they and we are God's mouth, hands and feet on this earth. We become such good channels of His grace that we become redeemers like Jesus. We take on the Family likeness because we have taken on the Family ways. And in the same way that Jesus gave all His glory to His Father, we also give all the glory to Jesus. That is exactly what it means to be a redeemer like Jesus is. And that is exactly what we become as we minister to others from the Lord.

"All this is from God, who reconciled us to himself through Christ, and gave us the ministry of reconciliation." (2 Cor 5:18). *"You will bear much fruit and your fruit will remain."* (John 15:16). For ever.

Licence, Law and Liberty.

LICENCE	LEGALISM	LIBERTY
Doing what is right in one's own eyes.	Obedience to rules and regulations.	Living by the prompting of the Holy Spirit alone.
Anarchy.	Rules direct me.	By Grace alone through Faith alone.
"Doing my own thing"	"Ought, should, must"	"Whatever You say, Lord"
I am sovereign over all my own choices.	The State is sovereign.	Jesus Christ is Lord.
Living by satan	Living under a curse	Forgiven.

Gal 5:16-19 (and I have quoted it below) tells of only three possible lifestyles that any human can follow: Licence, Legalism or Liberty. Licence means doing my own thing (anarchy). Legalism means living by and under Law. Liberty means living by the Holy Spirit.

I was redeemed from my anarchy when I became a Christian. *"Shall we go on sinning, so that grace may increase? By no means! We are those who have died to sin; how can we live in it any longer?"* (Rom 6:1-2). We then normally come under the authority of Law. But the Christian lifestyle is only to do the Lord's will. Let me explain:

1. The purpose of Law is to tell us we are bad (Rom 3:20), stop us getting worse (Gal 3:23), and to lead us to Christ (Gal 3:24). Law is the Divine *restraint* against anarchy (which was demonstrated globally during the days of Noah before the flood) and, since Eden, anarchy has been part of every human psyche. Anarchy (or Licence) is the definition of Original Sin.

2. So what about Law? *"For if a law had been given that could impart life, then righteousness would certainly have come by the law."* (Gal 3:21). Law can NEVER make anyone righteous. That's why God has now discarded it as a way of life, and has had to replace it. It was only a temporary stop-gap to curb the proliferation of selfishness and sin. Heb 7:19 *"for the law made nothing perfect"*.

3. Now that Christians are under Jesus, we are no longer under Law. *"For*

all who rely on the works of the law are under a curse, as it is written: 'Cursed is everyone who does not continue to do everything written in the Book of the Law.'" (Gal 3:10).

4. *"For I tell you that unless your righteousness surpasses that of the Pharisees and the teachers of the law, you will certainly not enter the kingdom of heaven."* (Matt 5:20). So how is that going to be achieved? How *can* our righteousness be greater than that of the Pharisees living under Law? Paul, as a Pharisee, claimed that, according to the Law, he was perfect (Phil 3:6). But then said that he counted that kind of righteousness as manure.

5. To accomplish that life of perfection, God has provided an alternative way of living – living by faith in the prompting of Jesus, or "Living by the Spirit".

6. *"Now to the one who works, wages are not credited as a gift but as an obligation. However, to the one who does not work but trusts God who justifies the ungodly, their faith is credited as righteousness."* (Rom 4:4-5). *"'Abraham believed God, and it was credited to him as righteousness.'"* (Rom 4:3). So, none of us are righteous people: *"But we have this treasure in jars of clay to show that this all-surpassing power is from God and not from us."* (2 Cor 4:7). We still have limitations and we still select sin rather than Jesus on occasions, but it is our FAITH that God says equals righteousness. The most righteous thing we can ever do in life is to put our faith in Jesus and His daily promptings.

7. How does that occur? *"It is written: "Man shall not live on bread alone, but on every word that comes from the mouth of God."'"* (Matt 4:4). That is, every *spoken* word that comes out of God's mouth (the Greek is *rhēma*, a spoken word). So, Jesus has promised never to leave us or abandon us, and He is standing alongside us, inside us and speaking to us all the time, giving us appropriate instructions in every instance of time. He has equipped us to do God's will through a living relationship that goes everywhere we go, and communicates with us at every waking minute of every day. Only God can live God's required way of life, and Jesus is the only human being in the universe who accomplished it, and therefore whom God approves of. That's why everything outside Jesus is sin, and everything inside Jesus is Life, and only accessed by Faith. The brilliance of the Cross is that it not only erased the past, but released

the Holy Spirit to dwell inside any human, and thereby let them know what God's will is at any moment in time. It enables any human to live like Jesus lived – in the permanent approval of God. It was very brave of God to do this for wicked people.

8. *"Consequently, faith comes from hearing the message, and the message is heard through the word of Christ."* (Rom 10:17). The Greek word for "word" there is also *rhēma*, the spoken word. So, that's how faith comes. Jesus prompts us first, we hear, believe it is He who has spoken, and do what He suggests. That is what "living by faith" is. And we Christians *"… live by faith, not by sight."* (2 Cor 5:7). *"For sin shall no longer be your master, because you are not under the law, but under grace."* (Rom 6:14). There is the clarity – *not* anarchy or Licence, *not* Law or Legalism, but *Grace.* There's the stark contrast. Either we are still living under law in our own strength or we are living God's much higher way of life, by His Grace alone. God hates compromise, and that's what I used to do in the RAF. Now I am living under God's Grace (trying to). John Stott preached a sermon one day entitled "God's Irreducible Minimum", which he defined as "By Grace alone through Faith alone". That is the Biblical truth and the Biblical way of life.

9. Thus, for the Christian, *"…**everything** that does not come from faith is sin."* (Rom 14:23b). That especially applies to things driven and demanded by Law. (I will try to work out where Law stands for the Christian in paragraph 11). Rom 14:23b is not God's *ideal* – merely a wishful dream that cannot be fulfilled by anyone. It is a reality, *because* the Holy Spirit is inside us prompting us to do the Lord's will every moment of every day, and providing the power and resources whereby we can accomplish it. Only God can do God's will. That's why He has provided Himself to enable us to live in the Father's will. *"For in the gospel the righteousness of God is revealed – a righteousness that is by faith from first to last, just as it is written: 'The righteous will live by faith.'"* (Rom 1:17).

10. We make mistakes, of course, because we are still very limited people who sometimes select our own ways instead of those of Jesus. But, for the Christian, the eternal consequences of sin do not matter any more, because Jesus has erased them all. Its punishment has been taken away by Jesus' Cross. Limitations don't matter either – they too are covered by the Cross, and complemented by the Body of Christ. It is *man* who

condemns, not God; *"Therefore, there is now no condemnation for those who are in Christ Jesus, because through Christ Jesus the law of the Spirit who gives life has set you free from the law of sin and death."* (Rom 8:1-2). God does not go around collecting errors so that He can clobber us on the Day of Judgement; all those errors have been and are continually being erased from our account by Jesus. God goes around collecting acts of faith, because *"according to your faith it will be done for you."* (Matt 9:29). So, if *God* covers over the multitude of sins, why are other Christians highlighting them and condemning their fellow saints? Someone has said that the Christian Church is the only army in the world that kills its own soldiers. *"If you bite and devour each other, watch out or you will be destroyed by each other."* (Gal 5:15). Following Jesus means that we promote, affirm, encourage, build every human being we meet, and love them into the Kingdom of God. Why are Christians trying to force other Christians to live again under Law, bringing them back under a curse?

11. So let me try to say how Law now fits into the Christian life. *"Is the law, therefore, opposed to the promises of God? Absolutely not! For if a law had been given that could impart life, then righteousness would certainly have come by the law. But Scripture has locked up everything under the control of sin, so that what was promised, being given through faith in Jesus Christ, might be given to those who believe."* (Gal 3:21-22). Law still exists, because the world is still full of sinners not submitted to God's Grace. Therefore, all of them (the vast majority) are forced to live "under law" and law is still the "schoolmaster" to drive them to Christ. Law makes everyone feel guilty, so that everyone can turn to Jesus for redemption.

12. All our actions still have earthly consequences (for Christian and non-Christian alike), which are inevitable; *"Do not be deceived: God cannot be mocked. A man reaps what he sows. Whoever sows to please their flesh, from the flesh will reap destruction; whoever sows to please the Spirit, from the Spirit will reap eternal life."* (Gal 6:7). So if I break speed limits, I get clobbered by the police (earthly consequence), but forgiven by God (after repenting and keeping short accounts with God). So the Lord, through His relationship and moment by moment communication, prompts Christians to follow the Laws of the land, even though they might be unaware of them. *"Love does no harm to a neighbour. Therefore love is the fulfilment of the law."* (Rom 13:10). Living with Jesus and obeying Him thereby makes Christians more righteous than non-Christians – they

live far beyond the minute details of the Law. So take careful note of this scripture: *"And so he condemned sin in the flesh, in order that the righteous requirement of the law might be **fully** met in us, who do not live according to the flesh but according to the Spirit."* (Rom 8:4). The contrast is very clearly laid out in Rom 8:5-8: *"Those who live according to the flesh have their minds set on what the flesh desires; but those who live in accordance with the Spirit have their minds set on what the Spirit desires. The mind governed by the flesh is death, but the mind governed by the Spirit is life and peace. The mind governed by the flesh is hostile to God; it does not submit to God's law, nor can it do so. Those who are in the realm of the flesh cannot please God."* So, legalists and anarchists **cannot** please God. Gal 5:16-18 gives us a brilliant analysis of the 3 ways of life possible for humans: Licence, Legalism, or the Liberty of the Holy Spirit. *"So I say, live by the Spirit, and you will not gratify the desires of the flesh. For the flesh desires what is contrary to the Spirit, and the Spirit what is contrary to the flesh. They are in conflict with each other, so that you are not to do whatever you want. But if you are led by the Spirit, you are not under the law."* So, we must not do our own anarchical thing any more, and living by rules and regulations under Law curses our lives. So how then can we live? Simply - live and walk by the Holy Spirit in the peace and prosperity of Jesus. Why don't Christians follow the Biblical ways?

13. There are going to be occasions when the laws of the land contravene God's immediate will in a given situation. Jesus encountered a number of these, encapsulated in the Sabbath laws written by the Scribes and Pharisees. And He simply broke them (Matt 12:1-14). What, Jesus breaking the law? Certainly! "Those are laws made by man not by God" He said (Mark 7:7). So God will always prompt us to follow the laws of the land where appropriate, but also do much more than following laws – because God's ways are higher than man's ways. He is, after all, the Judge of the whole earth. If we follow His will and ways, then we cannot do better in our lives or be more righteous. We follow all appropriate rules of man *and* please God, all by listening to the Holy Spirit and following Him. That is how we should live. Jesus is the engine that drives us – telling us what to do that's right and stopping us doing what's wrong.

My charity SIFT is there simply because of the Walk of Faith that I followed. Without my faith and obedience there would be no SIFT. And did it work? It has been marvellously successful. God has taken on what God began. I am only a passing entrepreneur and developer. SIFT should continue to be a work of God's Grace alone by Faith alone.

"Therefore, if anyone is in Christ, the new creation has come: the old has gone, the new is here!" (2 Cor 5:17).

"He (God) has made us competent as ministers of a new covenant – not of the letter but of the Spirit; for the letter kills, but the Spirit gives life." (2 Cor 3:6).

The Spiritual Battle

So let us look at the spiritual aspect of things on earth. Jesus said a very interesting thing in Matthew 18:18 *"I tell you the truth, whatever you bind on earth will be bound (is already bound) in heaven, and whatever you loose on earth will be loosed (is already loosed) in heaven."* I have translated "having been bound" (the original Greek) and "having been loosed" as "already bound", and "already loosed". What exactly is He saying? He is saying that the spiritual realm is controlled by what we do down here on the earth. God has already established the governing parameters and the spiritual balances. There is a spiritual bridge joining us with other people which passes through the heavenlies. So, if I am binding to myself a lustful spirit, then other people about whom I think lustfully are also becoming bound up by that same spirit. So, if I think about a pretty woman and start thinking lustful thoughts about her, then a lustful spirit hovers over her, and she will struggle to have a normal and proper relationship with me, and then with others. She will gradually become contaminated by it.

This may not be particularly obvious. So, by way of illustration, let me use anger. If I am incensed about someone else's behaviour and am angry over it (that is, I have accepted a demon spirit of anger into my soul), then I release (a demonic spirit of) anger into that person. They then find it very much easier to get angry back at me, to accept the demon spirit of anger into their own lives, and then to transmit it onwards to other people. If I bind a demon spirit of anger into my heart here on earth, the spirit of anger is given predominance in the heavenlies, and the person about whom I am angry gets caught up with that anger and cannot be released until I release him. See the contrast: *"A gentle answer turns away wrath, but a harsh word stirs up anger."* (Prov 15:1).

This is the way that demonic attitudes spread from one person to another. We "catch" them like we catch a common cold, but attitudes are caught *through* the channel of the spirit realm, did we but know it.

Matthew 18:18 reveals, as I have said, that there is a bridge between me and another person on earth which travels through the spirit realm. Whatever I bind in my own heart on earth is established and confirmed in heaven, and the other person cannot be set free from that bondage until I release that spirit in my own heart in relation to him. To make that clearer, he cannot be released from his anger until I get rid of my anger towards him. What *I* bind on earth is bound in the heavenly places, and if that binding of mine is sinful, then I cover the other person with chains from which he will have immense trouble getting free.

That is when the second half of Jesus' statement kicks in. Whatever I loose or set free on this earth has a corresponding releasing in heaven, and the other person is freed to be cleared of the negative within him. This is why forgiveness is so vitally importance in life. As is love, acceptance, affirmation, integrity, kindness, grace and all the rest. If those good things genuinely reside in my heart towards everyone I know, they communicate to others and set them free because goodness then predominates in the heavenly places. Other people can then be set free from their negatives because God's freedom wins the battle over evil "up there", released from my embracing of them "down here".

The order of wickedness is this: First we are tempted. Then we indulge. That binds a particular demon spirit into our souls. Then we automatically promote it (because we cannot help but do so – see the next paragraph). Then satan starts to win battles in the heavenly conflict.

We can see that personal victory in our own hearts must come first, because whatever we bind on earth becomes our master (exactly according to Romans 6:16 *"Don't you know that when you offer yourselves to someone to obey him as slaves, you are slaves to the one whom you obey—whether you are slaves to sin, which leads to death, or to obedience, which leads to righteousness?"*), and it then predominates in the heavenly places. It might occur to you that I am saying that, in the heavenly places, there is equilibrium between the forces of good and evil. But be assured I am not. God is infinitely more powerful and greater than all the forces of evil put together. The truth is that He has placed the heavenly battle in balance waiting for Christian people on earth to tip it in Jesus' favour. So what I am doing down here on earth governs the success or failure of the angels in heaven to bring goodness to the earth, because what I bind on earth binds heaven. Sinful Christians on earth release greater wickedness on earth. It's not only that when good men keep silent wickedness prevails. When good men keep silent or just don't bother, satan is released to extend his kingdom more and more. There is a definite outcome from all negativity – if you see what I mean. The predominance of evil on earth in any one generation is governed by the lack of strength and aggressive faithfulness of Christian people fighting the heavenly battle from earth. To put that as harshly as I can, it is *my fault entirely* that secularism and all kinds of other evils have surreptitiously invaded the UK during my lifetime.

As a man and a Christian leader who has lived mainly through the 20th century, what inheritance have I bequeathed to my daughter's generation in her 21st century? I regret …

We can see whether Jesus' words are true or not merely by looking at the results. Just take a look at the moral state of Britain at this time. It looks very much as if satan is winning the battle between good and evil. So, taking the principles of Matthew 18, what has actually been happening? Answer - Christians have been compromising privately with sin. Outwardly they may be good, upright, church-going men and women of integrity. But inwardly they are indulging in and enjoying the sinful things they see around. Others might look at their outward appearance, but God looks on the heart and responds accordingly.

Let me give you some examples:

Secularism predominates in our nation *because* Christians are being secular in their business affairs, rather than being Christ-centred, Biblically-directed and Holy Spirit led.

Sexual promiscuity predominates *because* Christian people are being sexually promiscuous privately inside.

Binge drinking has captured millions in the United Kingdom *because* Christian people compromise on drink and drunkenness in their own hearts and sometimes in their lives. Therefore they don't speak out against it. They may tut-tut about it at home, but they prefer not to make waves that could strike back.

Syncretism predominates *because* Christian people compromise over the exclusivity of Jesus. (To syncretize means "To attempt to combine the characteristic teachings, beliefs, or practices of different systems of religion or philosophy.") Tolerance may be a nice thing to have, but did you know that it is not a New Testament characteristic? It is used once in the NIV (Rom 2:4), and there it talks about God's tolerating us; there is nothing about us tolerating other people's erroneous and unbiblical views. Jesus said that no one comes to the Father except through Him (John 14:6). That seems pretty exclusive and uncompromising to me. All religions do not lead to God.

The **Prisons** are full to overflowing *because* Christian men and women have kept silent when ungodly laws have been allowed to encroach on our society. The law reflects the society. Ungodly laws reflect an ungodly society, and we have them because Christians have been cowardly and have refused to stand up and be counted for good. Therefore the increase of wickedness is fundamentally due to Christian ineptitude, inertia and compromise.

Materialism predominates in our nation *because* Christians love materialism as much as the world does. By our behaviour it is clear that we worship material things as much if not more than we worship Jesus. Test it for yourself: what would your reaction be if someone burgled your house, burned it down and your insurance did not cover it? Or wrote your car off and the insurance refused to pay for another?

Jesus said that it was out of the heart of man that all sorts of wickednesses emerge. So we have to look at the heart as the cause of wickednesses. It is clear that the heart of Christian men and women govern the heavenly victories, so the fact that goodness is not winning on earth is due to the fact that goodness is not winning in heaven, which is due to the fact that Christian men and women prefer evil to good. Sad but true.

So are *Christians* responsible for the wickedness in our nation? Certainly. Undoubtedly. Why? Because Christians are the only ones who know how to pray, and they haven't done so. They are the only ones who know about the spiritual battle in the heavenly places and are the only ones who can affect it. Non-Christians have no insight into these things and are full of sin anyway. And even if Christians are in the minority (they always are), their Jesus is so strong that only a few can change a nation by their praying and pure lives. Didn't Abraham save Lot and his family – and if he had persevered he might even have saved Sodom and Gomorrah?

I put most of the blame on Christians of my own gender. Men must always take the lead in all affairs of earth. If therefore Christian men are compromising, the whole earth will increasingly come under the influence of satan rather than God. This is certainly true of any nation and is demonstrated in ours in particular. How else can we account for the decline of a nation that was Godly and righteous at the beginning of the 20th century to a Godless secular and wicked nation at the end of the 20th century?

Richard Foster wrote a book called "Money, Sex and Power". He pointed out that these were the three major areas of wickedness for men (rather than women). That is why the three rules of the monasteries were and still are Poverty, Chastity and Obedience. It has been true throughout Earth's history. Clearly modern Christian men have been sucked deeply back into these three major wickednesses, along with the rest of the world. This is why I blame

Christian men for the state of our nation today.

So let us address the subject of prayer. Clearly, if Matthew 18 is correct, prayer must play a phenomenal part in whether the angels get the victory over the demons in the heavenly places or not. But clearly that prayer cannot be a surface prayer that only impresses the listeners. It must be genuine and fervent prayer from pure, clean and genuine hearts. God, who looks on human hearts, will not answer any prayer that arises out of hypocrisy. I have a few Biblical examples for our encouragement. Elijah prevailed over all the powers of evil in his day because he was a man of prayer. He stopped rain from falling for three-and-a-half years, and then by prayer caused it to rain again. In James 5 we read, *"The prayer of a righteous man is powerful and effective."* The Lord turned the captivity of Job when he prayed for his friends. It only takes one godly person to change the balance of heaven by prayer. How much more can a nation be rescued by many godly pray-ers? Indeed, prayer is so important that I have been driven to write whole chapters on it.

But prayer is useless without purity. God sees straight and rewards according to our hearts and not our words. Days of prayer must always be preceded by days of genuine and long-term repentance; otherwise we are wasting our time.

So what about women? The truth is that Christian women should be supporting their men, both in their man's behaviour and by prayer. Because of the state of our nation, it would therefore seem obvious that they too have abdicated from this most essential responsibility. A woman's vulnerability does not often lie in the areas of money, sex and power (women's major weaknesses are anxiety, fear and envy). Therefore she is seldom tempted with these major negatives, and cannot therefore be held responsible for the predominance of these three in our society today. But she can be held responsible for failing to uphold the integrity of her man or men.

Non-Christian people's lives can be protected from disasters by the effective prayers of Christians, waiting for God's timing for them to be rescued and saved from their sins and be born again.

Remember, whatever you bind and loose on earth governs the victory in the heavenly places, and then back down onto earth. *You,* Christian man or woman, are responsible for what happens in your nation. This is your hour. You have no other.

Welcome.

Welcome, Holy Spirit, friend,
You who are, but have no end.

Welcome, you sweet heart of God,
Treading where no man has trod.

Welcome, gracious source of Life
Bringing peace, combating strife.

Welcome, loving Master, who
Always brings us Life anew.

Welcome, precious, tender guest,
You who through whom our souls are blessed.

Welcome, loving heart, complete
For every human soul to meet.

Welcome, you whose heart is pure,
Filling us with strength so sure.

Welcome, drawing us to find,
Every source of love so kind.

Welcome, friend of Jesus true,
Blessing us with grace anew.

Welcome, you who bring new birth,
Fathering all for Jesus first.

Reconciling Spirit, come

Make my heart your long-lost home.

Welcome, Holy Spirit, friend,
You who are, and have no end.

Spiritual Warfare.

Ancient Greek Philosophers (Socrates, Plato, Heraclitus, and probably also Agrippa the Skeptic among many others) thought man was soul and body. Hebrews thought otherwise and said we were also spirit. The centuries have rolled by, and western Philosophers now think that we are Greek, and have stuck with the Greeks. That is probably because soul and body are observable in mankind, and, because most of them are not Christians, they have no idea whatsoever what "spirit" is.

Hence the death, or more probably the inadequacy, of most of today's philosophical rationale.

Spirit is what God is and where God is. Jesus' view: *"God is spirit, and his worshippers must worship him in the Spirit and in truth"* (John 4:24). Moreover, spirit is where all of God's other creation is – angels, archangels, and all the huge array of other beings out there that we cannot see. God runs His universe by spirit beings whom He has put in charge of every heavenly body (stars, planets, galaxies etc), and they are accountable to Him for the welfare of the celestial bodies they oversee. The fact that we cannot see them and have no mechanism whereby we can evaluate them, doesn't mean they don't exist. The Bible tells us they do, they are there, and that their task is to serve God. Also *"Are not all angels ministering spirits sent to serve those who will inherit salvation?"* (Heb 1:14).

There certainly is a bad spirit being in charge of earth. We are told quite a lot about him, and every human being on planet Earth encounters him and part of his task force every day. His name is Lucifer, the Morning Star. He was the greatest of all spirit beings, and was therefore put in charge of God's greatest invention – planet Earth. But Lucifer became proud, and thought he could run the universe better than God could (can). So he set up a rival kingdom, and one third of all the good angels decided to follow him, and became bent themselves. Unfortunately, satan (Lucifer's new name) remained in charge of Earth, and has, since the beginning of time, been trying to get mankind on his side in the battle that has inevitably ensued.

There is warfare going on in the cosmos.

Regrettably, we, humankind, cannot escape it. Indeed, we are at the focal point of it.

Unfortunately, our earliest ancestor, Adam, selected the side of God's enemy, and every one of us, since Adam and Eve's day, have been born on satan's side. God, who created us and loves every one of us, has had the enormous and costly task of doing something to rescue us from total disaster and death, and restore us to His beauty and joy.

God's rescue plan is wonderful, fully effective, and defeats satan's ways in every aspect and on every count. Satan knows he is a defeated foe in relation to mankind, so his never-ending task is to try to stop people from making any contact whatsoever with God's rescue. Daily he is diverting us from even hearing what God is doing, much less getting involved in it. Satan does not want any of us to lose our selfishnesses and hear about Jesus. Nor about the consequences of retaining the selfishnesses we were all born with. We are all involved in this warfare.

That is what temptation is. Which human being is not aware of satan's sneaky daily promptings to do what we know to be wrong?

There is no such thing as an innocent human being. Even the very youngest are naturally selfish.

Satan is a spirit being. So are we. That's why we can hear so loudly what he is tempting us to do. We all know that we have choice; every day we choose between what we know to be right and what we know to be wrong. Because of the weakness of our flesh, every one of us are guilty as hell. We have all chosen wrong. Not all the time, but regularly. Unfortunately, every wrong choice ends us up in judgement and condemnation from God, who is perfect goodness and perfect righteousness. And He is the final Judge for all.

God's rescue restores us to an intimate personal relationship with Him. That is when we become like Jesus, and obtain victory over the things that tempt us. His rescue involved the sending of Jesus to earth, so that mankind can have a role model on how to live on Earth in a manner pleasing to God. Simply, it is to do God's will every moment of every day. Jesus has provided the means whereby we can do that: He has forgiven us all our sins, replaced all Laws by telling us what to do at any point in time, delivered us from death (which is the inevitable consequence of sin), and sent the Holy Spirit into our hearts in an intimate relationship with God, who gives us the means whereby we can live victoriously in God's kingdom on Earth.

A Christian who has been born from above (John 1:12), been baptised in water and filled with the Holy Spirit, is now equipped to attack satan and his demons and take authority over them. Such a person has been placed in a position that is vastly higher than satan because he is seated with Jesus at the right hand of God in the heavenly places (Eph 2:6-7, but verses 1-10 are also relevant). We stand above satan and all temptation; Jesus has given us the victory over all of them. *"I have given you authority to trample on snakes and scorpions and to overcome all the power of the enemy; nothing will harm you."* (Luke 10:19). If you (or I) don't exercise that authority, who will?

All sorts of other wonderful things kick in too: *"For our struggle is not against flesh and blood, but against the rulers, against the authorities, against the powers of this dark world and against the spiritual forces of evil in the heavenly realms."* (Eph 6:12). *"For though we live in the world, we do not wage war as the world does. The weapons we fight with are not the weapons of the world. On the contrary, they have divine power to demolish strongholds. We demolish arguments and every pretension that sets itself up against the knowledge of God, and we take captive every thought to make it obedient to Christ."* (2 Cor 10:3-5). *"'Truly I tell you, whatever you bind on earth will be bound in heaven, and whatever you loose on earth will be loosed in heaven."* (Matt 18:18). *"Heal those who are ill, raise the dead, cleanse those who have leprosy, drive out demons. Freely you have received; freely give."* (Matt 10:8).

Did you get all that? Our weapons have divine power to demolish strongholds.

I have done that often. Have you?

Secular and Spiritual Work. – Part 1.

There is a vast difference between Secular Business and Spiritual, or Kingdom, Business.

Secular Business.

Secular Business consists of all the businesses that man has made and devised.

It would have started on day one or two after Adam and Eve were thrown out of the Garden of Eden, when, presumably, Eve would have stood in front of Adam, with hands on her hips, and asked, "Well, what are we going to eat then?"

So Adam had to go out and get food, plant and grow his own, till the ground in the sweat of his brow, and cook the plants before they could eat. All work from that moment onwards became *man* initiated and *man* run. This contrasted with the Garden, where God had provided everything they could eat, it was at hand whenever they wanted it, and all they had to do was to tend the Garden at the Lord's direction and without sweat.

So from then on, most institutions on earth have been man made, man devised and man controlled. What we have all been born into in every generation are man's institutions. They have all been man's initiatives, and they have grown more sophisticated as technology has developed. In school we were taught man's ways to prepare us to do man's works throughout our lives.

None of them were or are from God. God has observed what man has initiated, watches what man does with them, but does not put His Name to any of them. Indeed, God does not put His Name to any of the world. Earth, yes; world, no.

In accordance with the Genesis account of Creation, everything that man has initiated after the Garden of Eden is a dead work. All human works were initiated by dead men, are run by dead men, do dead men's deeds and will die. They are under law, belong on earth and in time, and are wholly confined inside those boundaries. Every human being is dead from their conception onwards. So are all his works.

There are three characteristics of works initiated and run by man:

1. They have a hierarchy. That is, there are authority figures rising up on top of each other.

2. They are controlled by economy. That is, without profit or accountability, they die.

3. They are under law. Laws govern every aspect of man's businesses or works.

These three ways are how we can identify man's works.

Because they have not been initiated by God, they have no "*zoë*" Life in them. That is, no eternal dynamic. They belong in time, and will die in time. Only in Jesus Christ is there Life. Christian works run very differently.

So how do Christians work in Secular Businesses?

To begin with, they cannot change the Business. No worker in Marks & Spencer can change M&S into, say, an engineering or an evangelistic business. So what Christians are forced into doing at work is to learn the Secular Business thoroughly, and carry out their work conscientiously, excellently, meticulously and with great integrity. Their *work* is Secular; their *method of working* is Christian – by the Holy Spirit. That is the maximum they can accomplish for God by working in the world. But, in passing, Christians ought to recognise that everything that their lives will have accomplished is to perpetuate *man's* institutions, promoted *man's* ways by doing man's business very well, and have contributed to the continuation of the Secular World into which they were born.

Many works have been started by Christians as initiatives from God. Schools and Hospitals are good examples. But because they have been so successful, the world has taken them over, secularised them and brought them under law. They have therefore become a mixture. Whenever that happens, the world can never take full control over them, and God still puts His inputs into them and uses them. But God dislikes mixtures, and any Businesses that are both secular and spiritual are never fully spiritually successful. For example, Christians can run a Christian school, but the children still have to pass their GCSEs and A levels (secular qualifications) if they want secular credentials to work in the secular world in their lives.

God also has His structures in His Businesses. But God's ways and methods are vastly different from that of the world, and Secular methods must not be used in Kingdom Businesses. God's businesses are under grace, and not under law. So let's look at them.

Kingdom Businesses.

A Kingdom business is defined as one that God initiates.

It will always be a new Business. It will begin by God calling a man or woman to be the person through whom He starts that work, and giving them revelation from heaven as to what God wants done and the means and location in which it is to occur. A church is a good example. Noah's Ark is a better one. Or the China Inland Mission (now OMF). Every Kingdom work will of necessity be a work of faith, and may collect a lot of opposition and some ridicule from outsiders. Initially no one but the person to whom the revelation came will see the need for it or how it is to be financed, built or perpetuated. So let's look at those three aspects of man's work, and see how they apply to God's works.

Hierarchy.

In a Kingdom Business, no human being will ever be in charge. Jesus is in charge. No human being will ever be in control. Jesus alone will be in control.

So what is the Biblical indicator of this?

Matthew 20:25-26: *"Jesus called them together and said, "You know that the rulers of the Gentiles lord it over them, and their high officials exercise authority over them. Not so with you. Instead, whoever wants to become great among you must be your servant, and whoever wants to be first must be your slave – just as the son of Man did not come to be served, but to serve, and to give his life as a ransom for many."* We need to see that God's way of doing things is diametrically opposite to and radically different from the way in which Secular Businesses operate, as Jesus so clearly points out in that scripture. There are no "ranks" in any Christian work. No one is in charge. No one has authority over anyone else. We are a body. One body, with all parts different, in place and necessary. But the Head is in authority – none of us are. *"And God placed all things under his feet and appointed him (Jesus) to be head over everything for the church, which is his body, the fullness of him who fills everything in every way."* (Eph 1:22-23).

So how can this work? If everyone is a servant to everyone else, how can the Business run? The Bible gives us the answer. Jesus is in charge, and His will can only be discovered by everyone submitting to Him and to everyone else, and being led in unity by the Peace of God. Everybody is promoting and honouring everybody else. In that way Jesus is glorified and the work becomes and continues to be eternal. Individuals have *responsibility*, but not *authority*.

Secondly, Kingdom Businesses are run collectively. No individual has the mind of God. 1 Cor 2:16 *"**We** have the mind of Christ."* Not me, but we. *"For in Christ all the fullness of the Deity lives in bodily form, and in Christ you* (plural, or **we**) *have been brought to fullness."* (Col 1:9-10).

Thirdly, *"Let the peace of Christ rule in your hearts, since as members of one body you were called to peace."* (Col 3:15). Or in the GNB, *"Let the peace of God guide you in all the decisions you make."*

It is very simple. When all the participants are gathered together, and after they have prayed, they know that what has to be discussed is the will of God or not by the fact that everyone is in peace over it. If someone is not in peace, they need to speak up, because without unity no team will ever find the will of God. Kingdom Businesses run by Unity, not by logic; revelation is God's way of working because God is super-logical. Mistakes can be made in Kingdom Business because people are not listening to one another, not communicating with one another, taking authority in place of Jesus, going an individual's way, or not using peace as The Sign of Kingdom alignment and God's approval. There is *no democracy* in God's works. Decisions must be unanimous or not at all.

Fourthly, the style of the Kingdom is facilitation and delegation in trust. Jesus delegated the whole future of God's Kingdom on earth to 12 very average men. He knew they would not fail because He was going to send the Holy Spirit down to indwell them to equip them for the task. That enabled them to hear God's voice and empowered them to do His will. What is of God succeeds; what is of man fails. So God did all sorts of wonderful things in the first century AD because He was set free through those 12 and their converts. It worked because God gave the life. 2 Tim 2:2 says *"And the things that you have heard me say in the presence of many witnesses entrust to reliable men who will also be qualified to teach others."* In other words – delegate all the time. God's

Business multiplies through those He has called. Everyone is unique, and God gives everyone a task and a role. But each individual is only used when he is in submission to all the others and, especially, to the Holy Spirit. God does it all, but through many people. The parable of the Sower (Luke 8) and the metaphor of the Vine (John 15) give us the details. *"Without me you can do nothing"* (v5) is the truest and most universal truth of all. God does not need our inputs, skills or our initiatives – only our obediences. God's Businesses take illogical directions, move in irrational and unpredictable ways and use the most unlikely people (like Gideon's 300). But they work because the Holy Spirit leads in His way and gives each obedience fresh new effectiveness.

Economy.

Man's businesses need to make a profit. If they don't, they fail. God's businesses never run for profit. Money is given by the Lord in order to be used for the purpose of promoting that particular Kingdom Business. It is not to be saved; not to be kept for a rainy day. Today *is* the rainy day. The money will never run out – like Elijah's widow's cruse of oil (2 Kings 4).

Law.

Kingdom Businesses are not under law, but under grace (Rom 6:14). Secular laws only apply when the Holy Spirit requires it, and He will be specific as to which apply. Otherwise, all law has been abolished for Christians (Eph 2:15, Rom 10:4). The presence of God in the heart of every believing worker is the guide and directive that applies in Kingdom Businesses. Jesus was perfect in everything by obeying His Father, not by knowing secular laws and striving to follow them. The Pharisees' and Jesus' methods of achieving perfection were utterly different. One by law; the other by grace. This contrast still exists between Secular and Kingdom Businesses. Jesus Christ is and must continue to be LORD over everything.

So what happens when a Kingdom work becomes influenced by secular ways? It loses the Divine initiatives because it reverts to man's initiatives, and the Holy Spirit moves away. We see this often in many Churches which we recognise as "dead". They do not have "life" as a Christian would recognise it, because all life is solely incorporated in Jesus. By taking control over God's

Business, men remove the control of the Holy Spirit. That is the inevitable but deadly consequence of "control". Indeed, the three ways in which man can kill a Kingdom work are: 1. Taking control. Or administering what is the exclusive flair of the Holy Spirit. 2. Misusing the money in any way, and not using it as God instructs for the work. 3. Bringing the work under secular Law. We can see this historically in revivals down the centuries. The first generation brought revival by the initiative of the Holy Spirit. The second generation killed it by administrating it. The third generation made it into a man-made denomination with hierarchy, economy and laws.

Secular and Spiritual Work – Part 2.

The Spiritual Man

The only people qualified to work in Kingdom Businesses are those who have been born again by the Holy Spirit, and to whom Jesus Christ is Lord of all. 1 Cor 2:14 tells us why: *"The person without the Spirit does not accept the things that come from the Spirit of God but considers them foolishness, and cannot understand them because they are discerned only through the Spirit."* Spiritual people should all have certain characteristics common to every Christian. These can all be summarised in the phrase "Fully submitted to the Lordship of Christ in everything." But the Bible narrows it down for us of which the following are examples:

1. *"The wind blows wherever it pleases. You hear its sound but you cannot tell where it comes from or where it is going. So it is with everyone born of the Spirit."* (John 3:8). So, every Christian should be "a free spirit". They are being led by the Spirit, not by themselves or by anyone else. As Jesus says there, the Holy Spirit is utterly unpredictable. So should all His servants be.

2. *"Those who live in accordance with the Spirit have their minds set on what the Spirit desires." "The mind controlled by the Spirit is life and peace."* (Rom 8:5, 6). I quote from Suzette Hattingh (Voice in the City): "I simply stood back and let God be God without interfering or trying to control the work of the Spirit."

3. *"Those who are led by the Spirit of God are sons of God."* (Rom 8:14).

4. *"We have not received the spirit of the **world** but the Spirit who is from God, that we may understand what God has freely given us."* (1 Cor 2:12). This tells us that there is a huge difference and exclusivity between the world's ways of working and those of the Spirit. *"Do not conform to the pattern of this world, but be transformed by the renewing of your mind. Then you will be able to test and approve what God's will is—his good, pleasing and perfect will."* (Rom 12:2).

5. *"The spiritual man makes judgements about all things, but he himself is not subject to any man's judgement."* (v15). In other words, no Kingdom Businesses are under human authority.

So, no Christian charity is under the Charity Commission's authority – unless the CC discovers they are misusing their authority or their funds. We can see this particularly in the low-key position charity Trustees hold in most churches and Christian works. Kingdom Businesses are not under law, but under grace (Rom 6). As a consequence, their lifestyle is far higher and fuller of integrity than any that can be found in the world. They are Jesus' *"slaves to righteousness"* (Rom 6:15-18).

6. *"In him you too are being built together to become a dwelling in which God lives by his Spirit."* (Eph 2:22). That is, Christians are One Thing, and should operate together to find the mind of God and do the will of God. For *"**We** have the mind of Christ."*

To summarise that, Christians should all be being led by the Spirit, should belong together as One, should bless one another, should promote one another, should release one another, should exalt one another, should listen to one another, should humble themselves beneath everyone else, and only in that way can discover the will and mind of God and fulfil His calling on their lives in peace and prosperity. Unity does not mean conformity. It means the richness of diversity through the medium of humility. Like Paul's Body illustrations in Rom 12 and 1 Cor 12.

The Human Example.

The amazing, supernatural and sovereign miracle of the grace of God is that it has enabled Him to redeem a totally secular human being and bring him into the Kingdom of God. God's grace enables the secular to become Kingdom – but only in individuals. God cannot and does not redeem Secular Businesses. No Secular Business can be resurrected – only destroyed (which Jesus will do to the whole religious, industrial and financial fabric of the world at His Second Coming).

With humans, the pattern and pathway of redemption is invariably the same. He challenges the total secularity in the individual, gets that individual to surrender the sovereignty of his life to the sovereignty of Jesus, and then takes him onwards and upwards. From then on, the way and the end are invariable and inevitable. The Holy Spirit gradually brings this human being detail by detail under the sovereignty of Jesus until there is no secularity and no self-direction left in him whatsoever. We are being brought to the place where Jesus Himself spent all His human life – *"The Son can do nothing by himself; he can only do what he sees his Father doing…"* (John 5:19).

Every single thing that a man does in his life in his own strength, with his own ability, on his own authority, or on his own initiative, is a dead work. That is true whether he is a Christian or not. The only things that have life in them are the things a man does on the initiative, prompting and ability of Jesus. It is black and white, all or nothing. Christians are moving out of the deeds of darkness (defined as using their own talents and skills) into the deeds of light (defined as allowing Jesus' directives to pass through them). Most of us live our lives in a messy mixture in the middle, like a butterfly being formed inside its chrysalis.

No Christian who reaches death is ever fully redeemed. No one ever fully comes to the place in which Jesus lived His life. But the closer we get to the pattern Jesus set for us, the more effective and permanent our life works are. The more that Jesus can acknowledge His sovereignty and place his ownership on our actions, the more eternal those actions become. *"Whoever claims to live in him must live as Jesus did."* (1 John 2:6)

The same is true of Kingdom Businesses. By definition, a Kingdom Business is one that Jesus has started. But as people come into that Business they bring with them the mixture which is a definition of their own personal walk with God. They nearly always contaminate the Business. Then, together with the others who are already working in the Business, they learn to change and surrender their abilities more and more to the Lord and to each other so that less is human initiative and more is God's sovereignty. Joining any Kingdom Business is a humbling experience to all.

When the secular world takes over a Kingdom Business – as in a hospital or school – the mixture becomes more obvious, and the contamination more abundant. But God will not allow the world to take over any of His works fully. That is why Christian inputs into medical and educational works are still available and why the world is incapable of taking those works over fully. God will always be able to inject miracles of grace into works He began.

In a purely secular work – a dead one that man has devised, built and runs, Christians can retain their Kingdom position, but The Holy Spirit surrounds them with a bubble of grace. That grace can never extend to the Business as a whole. That began as a dead work and will die as a dead work. The presence of a Christian in a Secular Business, however, enables Jesus to stop the Business going badly wrong – God blesses non-Christians because of the presence and prayers of the Christians, in the same way that the storm that Jesus stilled on Lake Galilee for His disciples also helped the "other little boats" that were with them out on the lake (Mark 4:36).

Christians must ensure that the world's "bubble", containing all the characteristics of man's work, does not encroach into a Kingdom work. When a Kingdom Business introduces the Secular world into its structure by becoming a Charity, it must make sure that the Secular rules and regulations that it is contaminated with take their proper place and do not take authority or a position of control off the Lord. The Charity Commission can never be the controlling authority in a Kingdom Business.

The key position that every Christian worker must come to as they work in a Kingdom Business is that they acknowledge and live the concept that "Jesus Christ is Sovereign Lord God Almighty over absolutely everyone and over absolutely everything." Christians (and therefore Christian Businesses) make God their dwelling place (Ps 90:1, John 14:23).

There is a freedom in all of God's works. There is fullness of joy, abundance, generosity, initiatives that really work, blessing, grace, wisdom and the happiness and liberty of heaven. Being involved in a Kingdom Business is an experience that makes us bigger than we ever were or could be, more fulfilled than any earthly thing, more effective than anything we have ever done before, released from the burden of responsibility without losing the responsibility, and living in a level of grace and fullness that is impossible to find or experience in the world. Jesus satisfies the human soul in every possible way, both by who we are and by what we do. There are no "oughts, musts or shoulds" any longer in the Christian life. Neither is there any condemnation for any of our limitations or failures. Jesus justifies us permanently before His Father. We fallible Christian people are already faultless and blameless before God (Jude 24, Phil 2:15). That is real freedom and enjoyed together as One Body of redeemed fallible people.

Selflessness.

The Holy Spirit gives us Revelations on top of each other. He remembers what He has told us in time past, so when He tells us something new that is based on something He has told us in the past, He reminds us of all the background at the same time. That enables His now communication to be as short, precise and pithy as possible. Putting another layer on His onion includes acknowledging all the layers underneath.

So, in communion one day, He told me something new, which will take me far longer to tell you than He took to tell me.

It is based on the revelation that He gave me last year that the nature of Jesus is absolutely selfless. Jesus has no ability or desire to exalt Himself in any way. That was His nature before the worlds were made, was His nature when He was here on earth, and is still His nature now.

In Philippians 2 we have this song of how Jesus made Himself nothing, took on the form of a slave and went to the cross. Therefore God has exalted Him to the highest place and given Him THE Name which is above every name, and that at the name of Jesus every knee should bow and every tongue confess that Jesus Christ is Lord to the glory of God the Father.

So, if God did not exalt Him, He would not be exalted. He cannot and will not exalt Himself. He remains the simple, humble Being that He demonstrated while He was here on earth. Everything that He now has – His glory, His power, His excellence, His majesty, His control over the universe – all has been given (and is being given) to Him by God the Father, and He possesses none of it. It is His to use at His Father's discretion, but never His to keep.

So, down here on earth and 2000 years after His death, He still takes no exaltation to Himself. Throughout the universe, the Holy Spirit exalts Jesus. So all knowledge of Him comes through the Spirit, and never through Himself. So then, if *I* do not exalt Him here on earth, He is not exalted. If *I* don't acknowledge Jesus as Lord, He is not and cannot be Lord at all in anything that surrounds me, and regardless of whether anyone else exalts Him or not. Because of His selflessness, He is utterly dependent on others to give Him the glory He deserves. That is awesome, but true.

When Jesus asked me to become a Christian, He asked me to surrender my self-centredness, give up my right to run my life from my own initiative, and rely implicitly on Him to "direct, control suggest this day all I design or do or say." I discovered (slowly) that that initial action of surrender and reliance on

Him is the same pattern that He has required of me every day since. It applied to different situations in my life as the years rolled by, but the pattern has remained the same. Paul told me the same thing many years ago if only I had listened to him: *"So then, **just as** you received Christ Jesus as Lord, **continue** to live in him, rooted and built up in him …"* (Col 2:6-7).

I understand perfectly now what the central programme of the universe is – to crucify man of his self-centredness. It is the root of all sin. Indeed it is the definition of iniquity. *"All we like sheep have gone astray. We have turned each one to his own way, and the Lord has laid on him the iniquity of us all."* (Is 53:6).

It has only taken me 54 years to understand fully what God has been up to in my life. He is trying to make my life like that of Jesus. That is, He is trying to make me as selfless as Jesus is. All the trials, temptations and difficulties that Jesus has allowed into my life have been the means whereby more and more of my selfishness has been challenged, surrendered and dumped. He is breaking the I in me down piece by piece until there is no self left in me and I am nothing. Jesus made Himself nothing. I am reluctantly becoming nothing. Reluctantly because I have resisted most of God's suggestions of self annihilation.

So if I do become nothing, on what can I rely for my life? Jesus, and Him only. Paul achieved it quicker in his life than I have in mine: *"I have been crucified with Christ and I no longer live, but Christ lives in me."* (Gal 2:20).

Let me make this personal, and then I will apply it to everyone else.

If Jesus does not exalt me, then I am not exalted. As a Christian, I am not entitled to exalt myself or promote myself or defend myself in any way. I am not allowed to tell of the good things I have done – only to tell of the good things that the Lord has done to me, through me and for me. So I have to rely implicitly on Jesus to be the beginning, middle and end of everything I do, and I must try to do everything in His name and at His direction. I am to be a nobody for ever. If God does not glorify me, then I am not glorified. If God does not use me, then I am not used. This complete selflessness has to be my desired and perfect way of life from now on and for ever. If you prefer me to put it another way, I have to live a life of permanent repentance, because, try as I may, self-centredness is ingrained in my psyche and emerges at every available moment. *"Humble yourselves, therefore, under God's mighty hand, that he may lift you up in due time."* (1 Peter 5:6).

So when I was in conversation with someone on the street the other day about their smoking, I was about to say that I gave up smoking when I was nine. But the Holy Spirit nudged me – that would put them down and exalt me. So I refrained from saying anything, and asked the Lord in an instantaneous prayer to deliver them.

In addition, if *you* do not exalt me, then I am not exalted. If you do not give a good report of me, then I have no good report, for I am not allowed to give myself a good report.

I realise that I am not perfect, that I have limitations and occasionally sin, just like you do. If you are aware of any of my limitations or sins, and tell others of them, then my reputation is soured by you. Yours is the choice. You can either promote me or destroy me. I have no defence, and I am not allowed to defend myself or justify myself. I stand alone and exposed before God and before the whole world. If God does not justify me, then I am not justified. If He does not come to my rescue, then I drown. So if you let me down and God does not cover or stop your criticism of me, I am maligned and denigrated for ever.

It also works the other way round. My task is to ignore your limitations and/or sins and promote you. If I do not exalt you, you are not exalted. If I give a bad or critical report of you, then I destroy your reputation in the ears of the listeners, and, through gossip, to the rest of the world. So one of my tasks in life, if I read my Bible correctly, is to love you, serve you, promote you, encourage you, pray for you and glorify you. You are unique in the history of the earth, and if God has set His love on you, then I must do the same. God does not criticise me; He forgives me and guides me onwards into His perfect will. That is what I must do for you too. There can be no rivalry between me and you, and no criticism. You are struggling with your Christian life just like I am with mine, so I need to help you along the way. I must be your reliable and trustworthy companion, your staunch ally, your protector and your promoter. That is all part and parcel of being a nobody, and part of the structure of the Bride of Christ.

Now let me take this from your point of view.

You are also being dragged along the same track as I am. The Lord is also asking you to be a nobody, and all the trials and temptations that you are facing are only to get you to surrender your pride and self-centredness and become more like Jesus.

So if you do not promote me, as I have said, I am not promoted. You have to exalt every other Christian, whichever Church they belong to. You will also graduate to finding yourself exalting non-Christians too. You will find yourself appreciating everybody for their uniqueness, their talents and for the glory that is theirs because they are human beings and because God has given them a unique character signature. You will find yourself praying for the non-Christians, glad to be in their company and helping them wherever you can. There is a Spirit of generosity and magnanimity about being a Christian follower of Jesus. In addition you will find yourself stopping all criticism of others. Stop the critics in their tracks. "I do not want to hear any more negatives about that person you are talking about." To criticise another human being is to be self-promoting. And as Christians we must stop doing both. Do not listen to criticism. If there is something you have against another, do what the Bible says – go and speak privately to the person alone. Do not try to speak to them through a third person (Matt 18:15-17).

So, if *you* do not uphold Jesus in the public place, He is not upheld. If you keep your mouth shut when He is disparaged, for whatever reason, you demote Him in the eyes of the world. Jesus will never promote Himself. He relies on His Father, the Holy Spirit and you to promote and glorify Him before men.

If you do not promote your Church fellowship, however grotty it is, then you let down your own body, because you are part of the Body of Christ. You must give total support to your local Church, both in your heart and with your tongue. All criticism is self exaltation, telling the world that you could do better than those whom God has appointed. That is not being selfless. Indeed, the Lord will not allow you to be promoted in your Church with that attitude. What you think you can do better than others cannot take place until you allow Jesus to be Lord over your life and for you to be dead to your own desires, wants and opinions.

The Lord's plan for your life, as for mine, is to destroy all self within you. You are not a great person, or ever will be. Neither will I ever be. I must be the servant and slave of other people, and must place myself below them. There must never be another person whom I despise, or over whom I feel superior. Even children. They too are to be promoted, loved, exalted, appreciated, affirmed and supported, both to their faces and behind their backs.

If the world thinks you are great, and gives you a Knighthood or makes you a Dame, you must not change. You still have to retain the common touch, to make others great in your sight, and to prefer them above yourself. You must never take any glory to yourself, for that will rob Jesus of His. Every exaltation and accolade that comes to you from other people must fly over your head, and never nest in your heart. You will never be able to agree with it, because you know who you really are. When Jesus loses His servanthood and promotes Himself above anyone else, then you will have the right to do the same. Never until then.

All this the Holy Spirit showed me in a moment of time.

This plan of the Lord's, to make us like Jesus, will be accomplished, because the Holy Spirit is at work within us all the time crucifying us and transforming us into the likeness of the Lord. When it is time for Jesus to marry His Bride, she will be fully prepared and every part will be like Him in this particular way.

"Whoever claims to live in him, must walk as Jesus did." (1 John 2:6).

The Flesh.

The Lord analysed for me (revealed to me) the truth about the Flesh. So first let me give you some background concerning the Flesh.

There are a number of lists in the New Testament concerning what it calls "the acts of the flesh". Nearly every list is headed up by adultery, and then goes on to expose idolatry, licentiousness, and general dissolute and decadent living. For those of you who are not familiar with these lists, here are a couple to be getting on with: Mark 7:21-23. *"For it is from within, out of a person's heart, that evil thoughts come — sexual immorality, theft, murder, adultery, greed, malice, deceit, lewdness, envy, slander, arrogance and folly. All these evils come from inside and defile a person.'"* Col 3:5-9. *"Put to death, therefore, whatever belongs to your earthly nature: sexual immorality, impurity, lust, evil desires and greed, which is idolatry. Because of these, the wrath of God is coming. You used to walk in these ways, in the life you once lived. But now you must also rid yourselves of all such things as these: anger, rage, malice, slander, and filthy language from your lips. Do not lie to each other, since you have taken off your old self with its practices."*

If any of you are like me, you will have read these lists, and avoided the negative indulgences they refer to, helped along by the Holy Spirit. So the Acts of the Flesh were characterised by behaviour. Some of them were acts and some of them were attitudes — like anger, rage and so on. But as we continued to walk with the Lord, He would have told us that all behaviour is based on heart attitudes. Flesh is both inside and outside. So, if I had jealousy or rivalry in my heart towards another person, that would emerge as criticism or manipulation behind their backs. The Holy Spirit's work inside me would have been to clean the inside first; then the outside will never happen.

Many of us think of the Flesh as the little (and big) indulgences that we regularly but secretly give way to, and there are certainly some Biblical examples of that perspective, include our lusts, our greeds, our tiny selfishnesses — all of which we are ashamed to tell of. We normally keep them very private. The Flesh certainly includes those, but it is far more than that.

What the Lord showed me was that the Flesh is **everything I think or do from my own initiative or in my own strength**. It is what the non-Christian world is doing every day. All the things I have been taught to do from my earliest youth, and was cemented in my education, that is the Flesh. School Education is me finding out what I am good at and improving it to my benefit, encouraged or forced into it by teachers (who themselves know no better). So, if I plan my day in the mornings and whatever else is routine in my own strength, that is the Flesh. Everything that I do and can do without the help or guidance of Jesus is the Flesh. If He has not prompted me and been with me in any action, I have done it in my own routine or ability, and that is Flesh. The Bible has much to say about it, more of which I will tell about in a moment. This may seem puerile and nit-picking, so let me explain further. "The Flesh" is me living an ordinary human life without Jesus. If that is what I do, my whole life is lost. I am a dead man; not living but merely existing.

Jesus lived for 33 years on this earth without sinning. That is, He did *nothing* on His own initiative, in His own strength or in His own ability. That may be difficult to grasp, but it is true. How then did He live? He lived only at God's direction. Even cleaning his teeth and going to the toilet were at the prompting of His Father – not just the "what" but also the "when". He lived in total obscurity (as God) for 30 years, at the end of which God the Father said of Him "This is my beloved Son, with whom I am well pleased." So, everything that we *normally* do and live by, Jesus did in collaboration with God. Those 30 years were not years of miracle; they were years of doing ordinary human things *with God*. He did nothing on His own or ever used His own ability or initiative. Even in the carpenter's shop. God is very good – better than any human – at living an ordinary life on earth.

Therefore, it is clear to me that the only Person in the universe who can live an ordinary human life that fully pleases God is Jesus. He has the ability to know exactly what to do at every point in time, and, because He is God and knows our characters intimately (more intimately than we ourselves do), He is the only person who can prompt us to live our lives in every way that pleases God. Isn't that obvious? In addition, His immensity is so huge that He can do the very same for every other of the billions of people that presently inhabit the earth – at the same time.

Everything else that I do, I do in my own strength and ability. That does not please God – it only pleases me – even though I might do it to try to please other people. Therefore, it is sin. Even eating my breakfast without Jesus is sin. So let me find you a scripture that gives us the principle. Rom 14:23b (which I have often quoted in my writings) says *"Everything that is not of faith is sin."* Everything. And, of course, Faith in what Jesus is prompting me to do is the key to pleasing God, because *"Without faith it impossible to please God"* (Heb 11:6). Through it I believe Jesus' promptings, and by it I achieve all sorts of supernatural things. The prompting of Jesus and faith to receive it opens heaven's door through my life.

Discerning where Thoughts Come From.

Since analysing what the Flesh is in this way, I have come to see much more clearly what is of Jesus and what is of me. For me to follow Jesus means that I must consciously do so. I consciously access Him – therefore I know that when I do so the promptings I get are from Him and not from me. The random thoughts that also come into my mind I accept come from Him, so I must consciously acknowledge they are from Him. So, when a random thought passes into my mind, I acknowledge it is from Jesus with a "Thank you Lord", and then try to go and do it immediately, dropping whatever else I was doing. The thing is this: Jesus knows everything that I am doing, He knows what I/we have planned to do, and He knows what God wants me to do with my hands, feet, mind, body at any point in time. From His perspective, I am an available servant to do His will at any time of the day or night – those things I have said I will do for Him. He takes me at my word, so chooses to use me to His advantage throughout my waking day, regardless of the things I am in the middle of doing or had planned to do together. So, if I make Him my planning guide, both the plans and the execution dove-tail together, and the whole is flexible. If He wants to change it in a moment of time, I must be flexible to change with Him. That's the way He lived on earth.

So I am understanding much clearer what is from me (I have calculated it and chosen it), what is from satan (bad, immoral, deceitful and evil) and what is from God (everything else). *"**Every** good and perfect gift is from above, coming down from the Father of the heavenly lights..."* (James 1:17). He is speaking to me roughly every minute, or, if He is not, it's because He likes what I am doing right now.

The Illustration of Peter.

One Biblical example is Peter walking on water (Matt 14:22-33). He was doing the humanly illogical and impossible thing. So long as he looked at Jesus, all was well. But when he felt the wind and looked down at the choppy waves, he realised that walking on it was not normal and was impossible and he immediately began to sink. He engaged his own brain, and sank. He cried to Jesus who said to him "O you of little faith. Why did you doubt?" In every circumstance, it all depends on whether I keep looking at Jesus and refusing to think or accept any other prompting, or whether I look or think logically. Rom 12:1-2 says that I must be transformed by the renewing of my mind. That is what I find it means – keep looking at Jesus and having faith in His promptings and stop thinking what I have naturally thought all the days of my life so far. Jesus is, after all, Sovereign over the whole universe.

I was a Conservative Evangelical (a born-again Christian who has not yet been filled with the Holy Spirit) for many years. That style of Christianity involves intelligence, education and self-control. I read the Bible and saw that it says "You shall not kill, lie, cheat, steal, covet, commit adultery and those kinds of things", so I thought "If that's what the Christian lifestyle is, that's what I will do." Therefore, in my own strength, I lived what I considered to be a good Christian life. But that was all of man. Almost nothing of that was from God. I am generalising here, but learn the scripture in Rom 8:13 *"If you live according to the Flesh you will die: but if by the Spirit you put to death the misdeeds of the body, you will live."* Do you see – if **by the spirit** you put to death the misdeeds of the body, you will live? If you put to death the misdeeds of the body by your own self-control, you will not only die, you will fail. God will not take away that which He has not promised or been asked to take away. You've still got it – whatever "it" is, and you will be fighting "it" all the rest of the days of your life.

What conservative evangelicals do is to ask God to rubber stamp their own efforts of righteousness, and their own behaviour patterns. So they live a life that is very little different from their nice neighbours, and think that, because they have been born again, God will rubber stamp all their own ideas and they will get to heaven where their neighbours won't because they are not obviously born again. It is utter folly: conservative evangelicalism is just as wicked and unbiblical as the philosophy that lives next door. There is little supernatural – that is, from God – in their lives. It will be a token only of God's matchless grace if they get into heaven.

So let me find some scriptures.

Biblical Examples of Flesh and Spirit.

Gal 5:16-18. *"So I say, walk by the Spirit, and you will not gratify the desires of the flesh. For the flesh desires what is contrary to the Spirit, and the Spirit what is contrary to the flesh. They are in conflict with each other, so that you are not to do whatever you want. But if you are led by the Spirit, you are not under the law."* Do you see? The Flesh and the Spirit are in direct conflict with each other. Any

Christian who does not find that to be true in his life is not living a Biblical or Godly life.

Rom 8:5-8. *"Those who live according to the flesh have their minds set on what the flesh desires; but those who live in accordance with the Spirit have their minds set on what the Spirit desires. The mind governed by the flesh is death, but the mind governed by the Spirit is life and peace. The mind governed by the flesh is hostile to God; it does not submit to God's law, nor can it do so. Those who are in the realm of the flesh cannot please God."* Please note the details here. If you are thinking ordinarily, as every other human being thinks, you are living in sin. The mind governed by the Flesh is *dead*, or, more accurately, *death*. The mind governed by the Flesh is God's enemy – hostile to God. It *cannot* please God. Joy Dawson has written a book entitled "Forever Ruined to the Ordinary". That is exactly what the Christian life should be at every moment of every day. Read that scripture passage again – the mind set on the Spirit only wants what the Holy Spirit wants, and lives in life and peace. So, change your mind.

Gal 3:3. *"Are you so foolish? After beginning with the Spirit, are you now trying to attain your goal by human effort?"* Well, are we? Does God class us as fools?

Gal 6:8. *"The one who sows to please his sinful nature (Flesh), from that nature will reap destruction."* I wonder, just how many born-again Christians are sowing and reaping destruction in their lives? It depends on the percentage of Flesh or Holy Spirit that governs their daily lives. Are we living "to please our flesh"? Reaping is inescapable. Guard your sowing!

Eph 2:3. *"All of us also lived among them at one time, gratifying the cravings of our sinful nature (our Flesh) and following its desires and thoughts. Like the rest, we were by nature objects of wrath."* So, just how much has the Holy Spirit had an influence to change our normal ordinary human life? How different are our lives from that of our neighbours – apart from us going to Church and they don't? Or, how different is my routine daily life different from what it once was? Just how many supernatural occurrences are there in my daily life?

Col 2:11. *"In him you were also circumcised, in the putting off of the sinful nature (Flesh), not with a circumcision done by the hands of men but with the circumcision done by Christ."* Has our change in behaviour been supernaturally engineered by Jesus, or have we tried to give up things ourselves, using our own initiative, and using our own self-control?

It is these things that have been made much clearer to me than they were before, now that I have understood that the Flesh is everything I do that is not from Jesus. Just as I was leaving Casa Mary Jane in Nicaragua one day, two Christian guys said to me "Maneja con cuidado" "Drive carefully". I made light of it and grinned at them. Driving away the thought came to me "Don't drive carefully, drive with Jesus." The difference? Driving carefully is me driving in my own strength. Driving with Jesus is me driving in His strength, and His direction, guidance, courtesy, promptings, kindness, covering, warnings, wisdom and everything.

"If you know these things, happy are you if you do them." (John 13:17).

The Old and the New.

Christians find it difficult to work out what of the New Covenant in Jesus removes things from the Old Covenant, and which of the precepts of the Old we are no longer obliged to follow. Let me tease this out.

The Old Covenant is, fundamentally, based on physical earth, so that, so long as we are still on physical earth, many or most of the Old Covenant constraints still apply to us as Christians. They were, after all, given by God, so many of them still apply. But I need to open up the boundaries to that below. I will also open up what has become new for us.

I am not discussing God's covenants with individuals here – just God's ways with mankind in general.

a. **Genesis 3**. Genesis 3 outlines the fall of man through Adam, and the initiation of death to him, the earth and the cosmos. The restrictions that God placed on Adam, Eve and the serpent still hold true, so long as we remain in these bodies. Our bodies belong to the old Creation, the first one. Because they have not been redeemed and resurrected yet, those restrictions still apply. Our souls are being redeemed, but our bodies will never be until the return of Jesus to earth. Therefore, women will still give birth in pain, and they are still subject to their husbands. Men still work in sweat (that is, with effort), and thorns and thistles still characterise our world.

b. The temptation to women is to try to give birth painlessly, and they will try to lord it over their husbands. Women need to remember that the New Testament tells all of us, men and women, to be subject to Jesus and to be subject to each other (Phil 2:3), and Eph 5:22 is specific *"Wives, submit yourselves to your own husbands as you do to the Lord."*- New Testament.

c. The temptation to men is to try to avoid hard work. Most men are still lazy.

d. None of these restrictions have been reversed in the New Testament scriptures. They are removed in heaven and the New Earth, but not here on this earth, and therefore still apply.

e. **Law**. The time between creation and the flood was a time of unbroken anarchy. Mankind did whatever they pleased without restraint. So, after the flood, God placed the restraint and restriction of Law onto mankind. The New Testament tells us that *"the law is holy, and the commandment is holy, righteous and good."* (Rom 7:12). It also tells us that *"Through the law comes knowledge of sin"* (Rom 3:20), and that *"the Law is our mentor (schoolmaster) to lead us to Christ."* (Gal 3:24). The point is that law was given to highlight and curtail evil and, in our despairing inability to fulfil all legal righteousness, it would lead us to faith in Jesus Christ.

Those Christians who say they do not still sin are denying the scripture (1 John 1:8), which says that we would be liars. So why do we still sin as Christians? The answer is simply that our flesh is still weak (Rom 8:3). Even though we have the Holy Spirit within us helping us and strengthening us, the draw of temptation is still very strong within unredeemed mankind; and Christians still live in unredeemed bodies. Those of us who have been redeemed are still undergoing the process of redemption. That is, they are still not yet perfect. We can overcome many temptations, but never all.

I will deal with the Lord's replacement of Law below. Meanwhile, the Law still stands behind us as our schoolmaster whenever we are tempted to stray. That applies to all of God's laws and all of man's laws too - modified by the New Testament below.

a. **Flesh**. The bodies we still live in here on earth are still unredeemed ones, as I have said. According to the Bible, it is virtually impossible for mankind, however long we have been Christians, to be strong enough to overcome all temptations – particularly our besetting vulnerabilities. Simply, our flesh is weak, as is our self-control. Everything that is done in the flesh is hostile to God, is God's enemy, and is an act of death (Rom 8:5-8). Everything that is done without God's instructions is flesh – and is death. That involves most of a Christian's daily life. That is why none of us can ever say that we are perfect. God has a solution (outlined below), but it is never perfect because of our weaknesses. In addition, old age multiplies our weaknesses and our vulnerabilities. No wonder Paul wrote *"What a wretched man I am! Who will rescue me from this body that is subject to death?"* (Rom 7:24).

b. **The World.** Everything that we live by in this world has been engineered by mankind. Particularly money. The Secular

> World System, which the book of Revelation calls Babylon, is all pervasive and dominates our very existence. That is, we all need money. The danger for Christians is getting involved in it – what Jesus called Mammon (Matt 6:24). Paul wrote: *"For the love of money is a root of all kinds of evil. Some people, eager for money, have wandered from the faith and pierced themselves with many griefs."* (1 Tim 6:10). In relation to the Secular World System, the book of Revelation tells us to get out of it: *"'Come out of her, my people,' so that you will not share in her sins, so that you will not receive any of her plagues;"* (Rev 18:4).

But because we are still in these bodies and therefore in this world, we are subject to the pressures and stresses of this world. The old still batters our lives from the outside. We do not need to be unrighteously attached to it, but it is still there.

The New Covenant.

So what has Jesus done for us? What advantage is it to be a Christian? How much does His redemption affect us?

The devil. Because Jesus took all authority over all the power of the devil, his influence has been neutralised (1 Cor 2:8). However, he has not yet been removed; he is still here. But for the Christian he has been placed outside of us, where before we had been saved, he was inside us. Some Christians still need deliverance from his place inside them, but that is all part of the redemption process. So, when he has been removed for ever from inside us, satan is still outside us attacking us. While we remain in his kingdom (he is the god of this world (2 Cor 4:4)), we can never avoid him or his influence.

> However, what the Lord has done for *us* is to give us all authority over the devil. (Luke 10:19). We are able to rebuke satan and all his demons. Our very word has power – just like God's spoken words have. It is part of our divine inheritance to take authority over satan. Jesus bequeathed that for us through His death on the cross.

The Law. Even though the law still stands behind us, it has been cancelled for us. God has replaced all law and laws. How? First the Bible says of the law *"The law is only a shadow of the good things that are coming—not the realities themselves."* (Heb 10:1). So, although it is divine and holy and perfect, it is a shadow. The reality is God Himself. So how has He replaced the law? *""This is the covenant I will make with them after that time, says the Lord. I will put my laws in their hearts, and I will write them on their minds."* Then he adds: *"Their sins and lawless acts I will remember no more."* (Heb 10:16-17).

This is really beautiful. The reality of all living in the universe is God. He is the solid of which all else is shadow. Therefore all behaviour that is real and permanent is what God says and does. And what Jesus has done for mankind by coming to earth and dying for us is to give us God's Life inside. The Holy Spirit tells us what to do at every moment in time. That "telling" incorporates all laws in the universe – both God's laws and man's laws. It also tells us everything we need to do at every moment in time, well outside the boundaries of all law. For example, He will tell us what to buy in the shops and when to go down there to do it – concerning which there is no law. He will also tell us what to say (or to keep our mouths shut) at every moment in time with every person we meet.

Jesus lived a perfect life on earth in the same unredeemed bodies as we have simply by obeying God at every moment in time. Jesus patterned our new covenant lifestyle for us. And when we fail, He forgives us; the cross is permanently available and effective for all time. So God is no longer counting our sins and failures (as man does); He is counting acts of faith.

The Flesh. Rom 8 and Gal 5 are very strong: the flesh is at enmity with God and cannot please Him. So, any one of us, Christians as well, doing anything without first consulting God, are sinning. Those deeds are death and are at enmity against God - even when they are nice and kind and helpful deeds. *"Everything that is not of faith is sin"* (Rom 14:23). It says "everything" and it means everything.

So, simply by listening to the Lord's suggestions in our minds and hearts, believing it is He who is talking to us, and doing it, fulfils everything that God wants of us. It covers the world, the flesh, the law, and the devil. God has made it so simple for us.

But the moment we revert to our own lifestyle we are in trouble. We will have been tempted by satan to do it without the Lord, it will be part of the flesh, and it will contravene the law. Those things still apply to us as Christians the moment we revert to our own way of thinking and acting – the way we grew up, the way we were taught at school, and the way we ran our lives before we became Christians. We are *being* redeemed – *being* saved. That redemption will continue to impact our lives until we die, when the battle will at last be over and we will be perfect kings and queens in God's heavenly Kingdom.

No male nor female. There is a verse in Galatians (3:28) which says: *"There is neither Jew nor Gentile, neither slave nor free, nor is there male and female, for you are all one in Christ Jesus."* This verse has caused controversy among Christians. First, the simple truth of it is that it is not yet so: there is still Jew and Gentile, male and female, slave and free. (Also there is still black and white, rich and poor, old and young). So that verse in Galatians cannot possibly be referring to this present world in which we still live. Those divisions still exist. So how does it apply? I would think that it applies in the Spirit. In heaven, none of those divisions exist at all. So, Christians need not regard any of those divisions as being valid when considering spiritual issues. But the realities of still being, for example, male and female, still apply on earth. Women are still to be subject to their husbands (or to leaders for single women), but have equal spiritual identity and ministry as the men. Men have to honour and respect the ladies. For example, God can and does speak beautiful revelation through women as much as men. It is a dichotomy that we all have to live with in this period of transition from the old creation to the new one, and will last as long as we remain in these bodies on this present earth. So, women can be in authority in leadership, but still need to be subject to their husbands. How to do that in God's peace is a battle they each individually have to fight, because both requirements still apply. And God is good to all.

Conclusion. I think the key to living in this dual state on the earth while the Lord engineers our gradual redemption is submission. When we realise that there is nothing we can contribute to our salvation, that all things are in God's very capable hands, and that the greatest man of all, Jesus, spent His whole life, both in heaven and on earth, in full submission to His Father, then submission both to Jesus and to all is the key to earthly peace. As we listen to the Lord's suggestions daily, we will always and only do what is right. Because we still live in unredeemed bodies, we live in a constant battle between the spirit/soul and body. Jesus is inside us with the Holy Spirit to help us gain our daily victories. Submit to Them.

Miracles.

Plagiarism means copying someone else's writings and claiming them for one's own. Now I am about to plagiarise. I have been reading C.S. Lewis' little books, and in the one called "God in the Dock" the first chapter is called Miracles. It was originally given as a sermon, and he wrote a whole book on Miracles which I read years ago and can barely remember, except that he thought that the Incarnation was the biggest miracle of all time. I quote him here, but plagiarise his idea - unashamedly

Just in case any of you have not read the chapter in his little book of essays, and are reading mine, I am going to share with you some highlights of his essay. C.S. Lewis had a very incisive mind. I love the clarity that he brought to Christianity. That clarity will be somewhat tarnished by my adding little bits to his writings, as well as taking away from them. You will have to read C.S. Lewis' chapter for yourself. I have given you all the keys to finding it.

Jesus said in John 5:19 *"The son can do nothing by himself; he can do only what he sees his Father doing."*

The first thing that I notice from that is that Jesus not only had a crystal-clear view of what God the Father did and does, but He also had faith to copy Him.

So what did Jesus see?

It is clear that He saw that the creation was wholly God's work, and that He was continuing to hold the whole universe together (things that we scientifically-blinded people seldom see or believe). That governed specifically what came next. "The miracles done by God incarnate, living as a man in Palestine, perform the very same things as this wholesome activity, but at a different speed and on a smaller scale." "The miracles in fact are a retelling in small letters of the very same story which is written across the whole world in letters too large for some of us to see." "Some of the miracles do locally what God has already done universally."

Bread. Jesus fed a multitude far in excess of 5000 using only 5 barley loaves and 2 small fishes. It is the only miracle recorded in all four Gospels. What Jesus saw His Father doing was multiplying on a global scale the incredible miracle of the annual harvest. One small grain of barley seed multiplies 18 or so times each year. That is 1800%. The world's annual multiplication of fruit and vegetable foodstuffs, using farmers with all of their various gadgets and abilities, is entirely God's astonishing work. It has fed mankind in all our trillions since Adam walked the earth. That is what Jesus saw with incisive clarity.

Therefore, in His faith, He did at a different speed what God the Father had been doing since the dawn of time.

In addition, the bread contained dead barley seed – cooked and ready to eat, not live and ready for replanting. Jesus multiplied dead barley seed (i.e. bread) for 5000+ people, adding to what mankind does to God's foodstuffs.

So also the **Fish**. They too were cooked and ready to eat, not live and wriggling, fresh from the lake. So Jesus added to the fish what man does to them (because He was also a man – THE Man), making the multiplied ones edible. God the Father is multiplying fishes in the vast waters of the earth at an exponential rate. Every day. Jesus did the same, locally, on a smaller scale, but using a different time frame. God in human flesh copied His Heavenly Father's style. He only did what He saw His Father doing.

What I have often called Providence in my writings, God is doing all the time. Providence is God using natural laws to do things that we can understand (we have the science) in the way that we have analysed normally takes place. We barely notice it was His doing, barely give thanks, assume it is natural, and even call it Nature. Actually we are calling God Nature. That is an insult – a blasphemy. Jesus saw with incisive clarity what His Father was doing every year, and copied Him. We call the feeding of the 5000 a Miracle: un-normal, un-natural, un-nerving.

But, since Jesus did that, His followers have been doing it on a smaller scale ever since. I have watched God stretch food prepared for 4 multiply into food received by 14. We are only doing what we see the Father do all the time and copying what Jesus did – if only we had the faith to make the same connection that Jesus made, and therefore do miraculous multiplications with great joy. Jesus is Man's representative in Heaven and God's representative on earth. What a Man! It is He whom we must copy.

Wine. Jesus at the wedding at Cana in Galilee turned 5 huge stone jars of water into the best wine that the master of the Wedding had ever tasted. "Fill the jars with water" Jesus said to the servants, "and give to the master of the feast." The servants became astonished. They knew exactly what they had done.

But how the transformation took place they had no idea.

What Jesus knew was that God is making wine all year round, year after year. He created the vine, created water (in the initial act of creation) guaranteed that every vine on earth would produce grapes, and arranged for its juice to ferment into alcohol so that the hearts of men might be made glad (says Psalm 104:15). The first recording of wine (and, unfortunately, drunkenness) was good old Noah – after he had done the extraordinary thing of believing God, building an Ark, and surviving the global flood. That was a long time ago, and there are many references to wine and its uses throughout the Bible, even Communion. God has been making wine ever since. So what Jesus did was accelerate what He had observed His Father doing. Jesus *only* did what He saw His Father doing. Therefore changing water into wine was absolutely legitimate for Jesus to do in the emergency of that hour.

Teetotal Christians tend to avoid this miracle. They think that Jesus implied that people could get drunk, especially on special occasions. That is never implied in the story, and their inferring is only a part of their prejudice. God calls some of His followers to teetotalism (especially those who were alcoholics in time past), but never forbids the partaking of alcohol. I have been both. In the RAF the Lord demanded that I be teetotal. Since I have left, he has released me from that requirement. We must be careful not to interpret scripture in accordance with our prejudices.

The Killing of the Fig Tree. As Jesus and His disciples were passing by one day, He saw a fig tree that had leaves but no fruit. So He cursed it, and commanded that it bore no fruit again for ever. Later on Peter remarked at how quickly the fig tree had died, from the root up.

All sorts of people have made all sorts of prophecies and predictions from this miracle, and I do not want to join them. But taking the rationale that C.S. Lewis introduced us to, what did Jesus see His Father doing that He could copy it? The answer to that is that God is killing trees all over the world all the time. Not just trees and vegetation are dying: the whole world is dying. We are also dying. We are children of our generation, and it is a privilege to live on this earth at this time; we do not have long. The food we ate today was already dead when we ate it. Trees last only a little longer. But there is no tree alive today that has lived from the beginning. All have died. It is the curse that Adam put on this earth when he ate the forbidden fruit in the garden. That disobedience brought death, not just to himself and his descendants, but to the whole earth as well. God is fulfilling His promise that death is the one thing that is guaranteed on earth. To everything. To all.

All Jesus did to the fig tree was to shorten what was eventually inevitable. Death was already incorporated into that tree, as it is in each of us. Jesus was fulfilling His Father's promise given to Adam that to disobey God brings death. Indeed, *is* death.

So what do I learn from this? That Adam was an historical man; that his disobedience was historical and recorded perfectly; that death is in us all because of his sin and our continuing sin. Jesus' action is a reminder that death is already working fast within us, and that He can shorten its inevitability if we are not producing the fruit He planned for us to accomplish. He said exactly that in John 15:2.

The Incarnation. C.S. Lewis quotes a rather nasty critic. "I saw the taunt that we Christians believe in a God who committed adultery with the wife of a Jewish carpenter." C.S. Lewis makes short work of that. In the following way, with my adding bits:

Every parent knows perfectly well that when they have sex and the wife conceives, they have absolutely no idea what they have generated, except that the result will be human. Is the baby male or female? Is it sound or special needs? What are its features like? What talents or limitations does it have? What is going to be its chosen pathway through life?

Every woman is born with about 900 eggs, and every man is generating spermatozoon at about one thousand an hour (so I have been told). Just how many people have ever lived on this earth? Trillions. Each female has eggs and each male generates sperm. *Every single one of them is unique.* There have been trillions upon trillions upon trillions of sperm generated throughout the whole history of the earth, each one unique. The possibility that you, reading this, turned out to be who you are is statistically infinite. No one can predict what any child is going to be like, given the immeasurable diversity and enormity of DNA.

But God says in Eph 1 that He has chosen us from before the creation of the world. So He alone knew what we were going to be like. That means that He selected the one particular sperm out of millions to enter that one particular egg that turned into you and me. He interferes with every conception that has ever happened on earth when He deliberately selected each human being. If someone wants to say that God committed adultery with Mary, He commits adultery with every woman who has ever conceived. The concept is nonsense.

But Mary was special. That particular egg of hers was the only one possible, in ways that I could never speculate, specially chosen from before the foundation of the earth. That makes her egg more important than her!

So what did Jesus see His Father doing that most of us don't see? That each human being on earth is a one-off, unique, special. There are no duplicates. Not only does that mean that every human being has been specially chosen and known from before time began, but that every human being is uniquely responsible for the life they have lived on earth. There are no human duplicates. No one has any excuses. No one can blame anyone else.

But everyone is also loved uniquely by Jesus. He who now knows the thoughts of every human being living on earth and the dead as well, is the perfect complement for every human's uniqueness. The greatness of Jesus is that He infuses and matches every personality perfectly, and is big enough to carry every human being.

Just as Jesus loved Peter, James and John, so He loves us one by one. That is why the gospel of His salvation registers still with human beings uniquely, and why that same gospel is the unique avenue for all to take to make heaven. It never grows old.

Healing. Every rational doctor knows that he does not and cannot heal. He can recommend appropriate chemicals or ointments that will lessen any bodily damage or hasten its health. But he knows that the body heals itself. Cut your finger, wash any dirt away, strap it round and maybe add a bit of disinfectant and in three days it is healed. Even if you don't wash it, protect it, disinfect it or strap it, it will heal itself in a week. Actually, God does the healing. In Him alone is life. C.S. Lewis has these beautiful sentences: "No dressing will make skin grow over a cut on a corpse." "All who are cured are cured by Him, the healer within."

That is what Jesus saw God doing all the time. Health and wholeness are incorporated into the created body. So Jesus' action in the eyes of disease was to speed up and localise what His Father had normally and naturally done when He made human bodies. Most of Jesus' miracles of healing came in response to faith in Him. Just as he had faith in His Father's works, others who had faith in Him were healed. The man let down through the roof (Mark 2) is classic. Jesus looked up at the four who had dropped him down, and "Seeing *their* faith … he said to the man, "I tell you, get up, take your mat and go home." He got up, took up his mat and walked out in full view of them all."

Even as I write this chapter, a little boy got his thumb accidentally shut in the door of my pick-up in Nicaragua. He was in agony and it may (should) have been broken. I told him, "Hold still and I will ask Jesus to heal it." I gently covered his thumb with both my hands and simply asked the Lord to do what He has been doing for ever, bring life. Within a few minutes the lad had stopped crying, could wiggle his thumb and within half an hour it no longer hurt. Thus Jesus said to His disciples: *"I tell you the truth, anyone who has faith in me will do what I have been doing. He will do even greater things than these, because I am going to the Father." (John 14:12).*

The miracles of Jesus starkly confront us all with our world view. We can't heal or do miracles like Jesus did simply because we have very bad and useless world views.

Communion

I have been attending Holy Communion all my Christian life. But yesterday I had a mini revelation concerning the Communion itself. It is so simple that it will barely take much to write it down. That should please most of you.

Jesus, in the upper room before He died, took the Passover meal that had been celebrated by Jews since the days of Moses and gave it a singularly new meaning and emphasis.

Indeed, there are many who have looked carefully at the Passover and found in it treasures about Jesus that have made thousands tremble with joy. The Passover is laced and intertwined with symbolism about the reality of heaven. The book of Hebrews gives us that clue. It tells us that everything God did on earth in time past is a shadow of the reality of heaven. Heaven is where the true and the real reside. We only see a glimpse of it as we study and meditate on its shadows here on earth. There are rich pickings from the Passover, if only we would take time out to discover them.

There are also rich pickings from Abraham, especially in his dealings with Isaac on Mount Moriah. Then there is the Tabernacle in the wilderness. Wow! That is lavished with divine beauty and significance. Moses told about it twice in Exodus. The first time was to write down exactly what God showed him in his visit to heaven. The second was to tell exactly how it turned out on earth. The earthen Tabernacle (or Tent) powerfully exalts the beauty of the depths of the riches of the wisdom, love and redemption of the God who cares for all mankind.

The Passover is a picture – a shadow – of the reality of which Jesus is the centre. So Jesus held His last supper with His disciples at Passover. Of all the rich symbolism of the Lord that still resides in the Passover, Jesus picked out only two. He highlighted bread and wine.

"This is my body" He said of the first, and *"This is my blood"* He said of the second.

The Christian church throughout the ages has made much of those simple words. And many have divided on their meaning. I have no intention of commenting either way on any of these divisions. I only want to pick out a few things that the Lord has emphasised to me down through my years.

So let's take the bread. *"This is my body"*. Now the Body of Christ comes in two forms. The first was His physical body that was crucified on the cross, and, now, His spiritual body here on earth and later in heaven. The second is the Christian Church – the Body of Christ – consisting of all believing Christians throughout the world and throughout the ages.

The first was crucified on Mount Moriah outside Jerusalem 2000 years ago. *"This is my body which is broken for you."* That was the ultimate sacrifice of the God who loves and cares for mankind. Jesus was broken in every sense and aspect of that word, showing just how much God is prepared to suffer to bring mankind back into companionship and relationship with Him. Jesus' broken body broke satan, sin, law and death in God's sight for ever. Believers are redeemed from everything that would hinder their relationship with the Father.

So when Jesus in John 6:53 said *"'Very truly I tell you, unless you eat the flesh of the Son of Man and drink his blood, you have no life in you.'"*, He qualified that in verse 63 by saying that those words are *spirit*, not flesh. The Spirit brings life; the flesh counts for nothing. We draw from his eternal resources every day (in the same way that we require food every day), from which we get forgiveness for all our failures and heavenly strength to do His will.

The second Body (Christians) is being broken and crucified daily. Every individual Christian and every representation of the Body of Christ is guaranteed crucifixion. Our identification with Jesus is such that we have to be like Him in all things. Including death. We have to die to our selves, our own desires and wishes, our own securities and ambitions. Indeed, God insists that we all come to the place where, like Jesus, we have nothing left in this world but Him. It is the ultimate identification for us all. So when I lay down my life for all of you, and you all do for me, we crucified people bring Jesus down amongst us as sovereign Lord over us all. That *is* the unity of the Spirit in the bond of peace (Phil 2). Psalm 116:15 says, *"Precious in the sight of the Lord is the death of his faithful servants."* And not just physical death at the end of our lives.

So every time I take the bread, I am saying to myself (being part of the Body of Christ), that I am willing to die for Him and you. The bread is broken, the Body of Christ is being broken, and I am in the process of being eternally and completely broken. I *"proclaim the Lord's death until he comes."* And if I take it weekly, I remind myself weekly that Christianity is a faith of absolute and eternal sacrifice, of which I am a joyful participant and a willing volunteer. Christianity is a Living faith of death. Death to the world, the flesh and the devil, especially as those three things are found in me.

But it is also a death towards other people; that is, we must die for each other. In 1 Cor 11:27-30, Paul says: *"Therefore, whoever eats the bread or drinks the cup of the Lord in an unworthy manner will be guilty of sinning against the body and blood of the Lord. A man ought to examine himself before he eats of the bread or drinks of the cup. For anyone who eats and drinks without recognising the body of the Lord eats and drinks judgement on himself. That is why many among you are weak and sick, and a number of you have fallen asleep* (that is, died.)"

The key to understanding this is *"recognising the body of the Lord."* That is, recognising or discerning the Body of Christ, the Christian Church. We cannot partake of the communion unless we recognise that we are part of the whole Body of Christ, that we are to be slaves to every other Christian, that we are to die to ourselves, and that we are to lay down our lives for each other. Just like Jesus laid down His life for us. Do we have a grudge against another Christian? Then put it right *before* we partake of the bread or the wine. Be cleansed first by putting it right with our brother or sister. Jesus forgives *repentant* sinners.

Unless we discern this as we eat, we bring judgement on ourselves. Those who don't recognise it bring disaster on themselves – weakness, sickness and death. That which God designed to bring glorious life in great abundance will actually bring terrible disaster. To individual Christians. And it will be a self-inflicted wound.

So let's look at the second symbol – the wine. This, Jesus said, was His blood. *"This cup is the new covenant in my blood."*

The blood is the Covenant. The book of Hebrews gives us many other purposes for the blood, and tells how it replaces the Old Testament shadows. But let's just focus simply on the one thing that Jesus said that the blood did and the wine symbolises. It is the New Covenant between God and mankind.

Most other covenants failed because all mankind are failures. But this covenant, the new one, is made between God and Jesus, not God and man. Jesus never failed and will never fail. Because He became a man and never failed as a man, God's new covenant will never fail with all of mankind. For all of us failures, to be "in Christ" is to belong in the new covenant. That's why the New Testament highlights and cries out "in Christ" so many times. To be "in Christ" is to participate in forgiveness, reconciliation, the indwelling of the Holy Spirit, and all the blessings of redemption.

It is a Covenant in reality from God that confirms and makes concrete the whole of the New Testament. All the promises of God in there are Yes and Amen for every believer (2 Cor 1:20). God has wiped away every sin, every hindrance to knowing Him, every obstacle from hell or earth that would get in the way, and is the guarantee that all three members of the Trinity would be with us and in us every moment of every day of the rest of our lives and on into eternity. That is God's promise (His Covenantal agreement) to every believer in Jesus. Ratified in blood. Christianity is a Living faith of Life.

So when we drink the wine, *remember* the Covenant. All darkness has been dealt with; all light has come.

Jesus told us to remember this every time we eat and drink. The symbols are so simple and we do them every day. God did it this way because nearly every Old Testament Covenant from God to man was not remembered by man and abandoned. God was enabling us to remember that this New One, the best of them all, would never be forgotten by any of us – or abandoned.

The bread is the healing and the reconciling of all things. Jesus' broken body brings healing and redemption to every individual, and *our* brokenness brings ongoing healing and reconciliation to the whole Body of Christ, and from there to the rest of mankind. *Christianity is a living faith of death.*

The wine is the Covenant. God will *never forget* the beautiful and glorious thing He has accomplished to bring reconciliation and to bring a hostile and rebellious mankind back into a magnificent and eternal relationship with Him. *Christianity is a living faith of Life.* So, regularly, re-commit to *your* side of the new Covenant.

Fine-Tuning in the Bible.

At the time of writing I have been a Christian for 61 years. By this time I should know my Bible well, and I do. But that knowledge is general. That is, if you asked me where a passage is in the Bible, I would probably be able to tell you. Sometimes I can supply the book, chapter and verse. Most times I can give you the book and chapter, and for obscure passages I can give you the book. I owe this knowledge to the Holy Spirit (of course) but also to the fact that I was a Bible Teacher at Upcott for 30 years, mainly to children and teenagers. But you will all know that the teacher has to know far more about their subject than the students – just in case a troublesome or enquiring mind asks awkward questions. Like a carpenter who knows his tools, I also had to know my Bible very well. That knowledge has stayed with me ever since, and, of course, increased over the years.

Listening to sermons is interesting for me. I fill in all the Bible quotes in my mind, and that serves to remind me of where everything is. I also get a Bible verse on my computer daily, and that is really good.

However, the Lord very seldom talks to me through my vast Bible knowledge. Occasionally the stories serve as illustrations, especially in counselling or prophecies. But background knowledge of the Bible contents is very seldom used by the Holy Spirit to talk to me.

So what does? Details. The Lord talks through details. Little verses here and there, or parts of verses get highlighted and applied by the Lord to my life. It's the fine-tuning that applies in daily living.

Why? I believe that, in the inspiration to the writers of the Bible by God, a miracle took place. Whether the writers were aware of it or not does not matter. Every verse is a window to the Spirit realm. A door. God is enormous enough to say *anything* to *anyone* through *any* verse. If we were to use human logic in analysing this phenomenon, it would fail; it is not logical. God can say (and has regularly said) many very appropriate things to me through verses that have no logical connection with what has been written. But once we have become familiar with the way God communicates with us (by thoughts in the mind and confirmation in the heart – that is, by Light and Life), all kinds of daily guidance, correction, direction and help come from the most bizarre of locations. I must be fully expectant in every working day to be spoken to by the Lord in the "daily round and common task" in all kinds of ways and using all kinds of methods.

Using the fine-tuning of scripture is a normal and common way of being spoken to by the Lord. Not using Bible knowledge; but using the Bible. Not using my learning and abilities; but still using parts of the written word apparently randomly. Nothing of me; everything by and from the Holy Spirit.

Having Bible knowledge is a human activity and can be useful in a human context (like teaching, for example). But that is not the way *God* works. God still speaks to me today in exactly the same manner that He spoke to me when I was a young, green and very ignorant Christian. The key issue is Life. Heavenly Life and heavenly Light come together (John 1:4); there is no duplicating it on earth; there is no substitute for it; human age or Christian experience is of no value at all in helping to hear God's voice. The youngest Christian has just as much revelation as an ancient one, and just as much authority in proclaiming it as his/her Minister. We are all equal in God's sight; no one is more important than anyone else. Only Jesus is important. No one else. That is true both on earth and in heaven, on both sides of death.

I suppose that the only value in being an older Christian is that our experience in hearing the Lord talk to us enables us to step out in faith quicker when He talks today. As a young Christian, I was not sure that the thought that came into my mind was Him speaking. Now I hesitate less in believing. Blessed is the young person who hears, believes and acts immediately.

The key to remaining faithful throughout our decades is very simple: one day at a time. Today – keep listening, keep obeying, keep confessing; never put anything off to tomorrow. Fine-tune your relationship all the time. Keep sweet with Jesus today.

Epilogue.

Cauliflowers are tasty. That is the major reason why we eat them. But tucked inside them and out of sight are all sorts of nutrients, vitamins and elements that do our body good in an unseen but very effective way. We eat things we enjoy eating. But underneath our body is telling us (through our taste-buds) what it needs to remain healthy. Some like savoury – some like spicy – some like sweet. We are all unique.

It is the same with the Word of God. The Word, as I wrote in the Prologue, is from the Bible. The written Word is not, comparatively, very important; it is the *spoken* Word that is crucial. The spoken and living Word is Jesus in all His wisdom, beauty and grace that we can glean from our Bibles. What is *Living* is the key. And only Jesus really Lives.

This little book takes us underneath the written Word of God. What the Bible *says* is only the start of what it *does*. Tucked inside it is the Holy Spirit, unseen, hidden, who brings us cleansing, insights, healings and transformations as we read it, like the nutrients in cauliflowers. The Bible is not Flesh: it is Spirit. And it must be read in the Spirit, not in the Flesh.

Many of the chapters in this book dig underneath the simple, written Word. That is a good description of Revelation. Revelation is just another word for God giving us insight that can never be gleaned from simple reading, using our brains. Revelation is not surface – it is deep down underneath, where God lives, loves, listens and laughs.

So, hopefully, you will have gained insights from this book that you never knew before. They were all new to me when God gave them to me. God will multiply those insights to you as you continue to walk with Him. I selected these revelations from among all my essays, and put them under the heading of "Bible Teaching". I hope you have been helped by them all.

Now go and glean more new revelations for yourself, then give them away to others.

About the author

Dick Bell was born in Kenya of a British family. His major love was aeroplanes, and, after his secondary schooling at Rossall in the UK, joined the RAF as a pilot. He became a Christian as a cadet at the RAF College Cranwell. He left the RAF after 20 years and became the main Bible Teacher at a Christian Conference Centre in Devon called Upcott, where he taught mainly children and teenagers for 26 years. He is married with one daughter and two grandsons. During his time at Upcott he took part in four Hovercraft expeditions on appropriate rivers across the world, under the leadership of Mike Cole OBE. Following the last expedition to Nicaragua, in 2000 he was called by God to take up full-time Missionary work there, where he founded the UK charity SIFT. His Missionary remit was four-fold – Initiate, Develop, Establish, Delegate. That enabled him to hand over the charity and begin a final new agricultural work on the Island of Ometepe in Nicaragua, where he also founded a new Church. He was prompted to write all the chapters in the Two-trees Series of books by the Holy Spirit since becoming a commuting Christian Missionary. He was granted an MBE in 2014 for his work in the Third World.

9 798557 882439